Africa's Cultural Prince, Dr. A.A.Y. Kyerematen of Ghana

Dr. A.A.Y. Kyerematen of Ghana. Courtsey of Nana Osei Kyerematen.

Africa's Cultural Prince, Dr. A.A.Y. Kyerematen of Ghana

Founder and Founding Director of the National Cultural Centre of Ghana

A. B. Assensoh
Yvette M. Alex-Assensoh

Foreword by H.E. John Agyekum Kufuor
Former President of Ghana

HAMILTON BOOKS
AN IMPRINT OF
ROWMAN & LITTLEFIELD
Lanham • Boulder • New York • London

Published by Hamilton Books
An imprint of The Rowman & Littlefield Publishing Group, Inc.
4501 Forbes Boulevard, Suite 200, Lanham, Maryland 20706
www.rowman.com

86-90 Paul Street, London EC2A 4NE, United Kingdom

British Library Cataloguing in Publication Information Available

Library of Congress Cataloging-in-Publication Data

Names: Alex-Assensoh, Yvette M., author. | Assensoh, A. B., author.
Title: Africa's cultural prince, Dr. A.A.Y. Kyerematen of Ghana : founder and founding director of the National Cultural Centre of Ghana / Yvette M. Alex-Assensoh, Akwasi B. Assensoh ; foreword by John Agyekum Kufuor.
Description: Lanham : Hamilton Books, an imprint of Rowman & Littlefield, [2023] | Includes bibliographical references.
Identifiers: LCCN 2023032057 (print) | LCCN 2023032058 (ebook) | ISBN 9780761873860 (paperback) | ISBN 9780761873877 (epub)
Subjects: LCSH: Kyerematen, A. A. Y. | Ethnologists—Ghana—Biography.
    Classification: LCC GN21.K94 A54 2023 (print) | LCC GN21.K94 (ebook) |
DDC 301.092 [B]—dc23/eng/20230830 LC record available at https://lccn.loc.gov/2023032057LC ebook record available at https://lccn.loc.gov/2023032058

∞™ The paper used in this publication meets the minimum requirements of American National Standard for Information Sciences—Permanence of Paper for Printed Library Materials, ANSI/NISO Z39.48-1992.

This book is dedicated to two important Kyerematen Family members: Mrs. Victoria Kyerematen (née Wesling) of Kumasi, the beloved widow of Dr. A. A. Y. Kyerematen of blessed memory. Currently aged over 100 years, she is an embodiment of affection and unlimited respect, hence some of us choose to call her Lady Victoria, in whose honor a very well-run hotel in the capital of Ghana, Accra, is named as "Victoria Hotel." We lodged there, with a lot of satisfaction, when completing research in Ghana for this publication.

&

Mrs. Bridget Kyerematen-Darko (1958-2016), educated at Ghana's famous Achimota College, she subsequently earned academic degrees and other credentials from Kwame Nkrumah University of Science and Technology (KNUST), Kumasi, as well as University of Ghana and Harvard University, USA; she died tragically as a result of wounds she suffered from the December 2016 La (Accra) gas station explosion. May she rest in perfect peace!

Contents

Foreword

The Supremacy of Culture in Ghana

Leadership, depending on which type or variation, has always moved human societies to desired and, sometimes, very undesired (or even sorrowful) ends. Therefore, when it is said axiomatically that every group of people gets the leader they deserve, it simply means the character and cultural upbringing of that leader could be reflective of the people; indeed, it can also be in the sense of family, clan, community, nation and businesses.

However, it cannot be solely the case that every group of people always deserves the leader they have. This is particularly so, as leaders could come by imposition and would not reflect the cultural dynamics of the larger interest. That, indeed, is the reason that very peaceful people in many places have been plunged into violent conflicts and wars by those, whose ambitions and characters were at variance with their constituents. The political history of Ghana has many pointers to this, a history of which USA-based Professors A.B. Assensoh and Yvette M. Alex-Assensoh, for example, have over the years worked hard to preserve, hence I feel delighted to provide this Foreword to their book on one of Africa's foremost cultural heroes and scholars, Dr. Alexander Atta Yaw ("A.A.Y.") Kyerematen of Ghana.

If we, however, look at Ghana's immediate post-Independence times and notwithstanding the political momentum that shepherded the country into self-determination, there emerged a soft power particularly in Kumasi where certain personalities of leadership stature emerged. Outstanding among them included Dr. Kyerematen before he became one of the national figures of Ghana's first cultural renaissance.

BRIEF BIOGRAPHICAL ANECDOTE

The young Kyerematen was born and bred in Kumasi and, as we know, he showed academic brilliance very early at Adisadel College in Cape Coast, where he was appointed Head Perfect and later continued to study at Fourah Bay College in Sierra Leone. Subsequently, he left for the United Kingdom to study at Durham University before he studied at Oxford and Cambridge Universities, thereby eventually earning his Doctor of Philosophy (D. Phil) degree in Anthropology.

When Dr. Kyerematen returned to Kumasi with his academic accomplishments, he had a plan to impact the cultural evolution in the building of what he initially named as the Asante Cultural Centre. It was not, however, just a cultural center but one that was attached to the famous Race Course in Bantama and a Zoo, which were previously not part of the landscape in Asante and most of Ghana, as indeed the concept was very little known in Sub-Saharan Africa. Before plunging his energies into the Asante Cultural Centre, which the first President of Ghana (Kwame Nkrumah) got interested in and eventually turned into the National Cultural Centre, Kyerematen became the first Ghanaian Town Clerk of the Kumasi City Council.

Indeed, growing up in the 1940s and into the 1950s were exciting for many of my generation, especially those of us who were in search of intellectual stimulation; we wanted by all means to get into the corridors of where some of the giants of our imagination and movement had been: Oxbridge and some of England's 'rose' universities. All of the foregoing nuances fashioned Dr. Kyerematen into an eminent role model in the country, especially among the youth. That was the first layer through which I got to know him, but he was also of the Aduna Clan, just as was my own Apagyafie; therefore, by Asante custom, we were distantly related to this great cultural hero, who carried himself with dignity and was easily approachable. He was very connected to the Manhyia Palace, where the Asantehene, Otumfuo Sir Osei Agyeman Prempeh II was his mentor; as the King of Asante, he was interested in preservation of the cultures and customs of his people, and found in Dr. Kyerematen an intellectual collaborator.

The mentorship role the late Asantehene provided for him aside, Dr. Kyerematen's family also had impact in the Asantehene's courtyard as—together with the Abenasehene—they were in charge of the wall robe and cabinet. This connection certainly influenced Dr. Kyerematen, who wrote several published essays of the functional values, including *Regalia for an Ashanti Durbar* and, in 1964, would extend that into the Longman-published book, *Panoply of Ghana*, which was initially planned to be issued to coincide with the visit of Queen Elizabeth II to Ghana in early 1960.

THE GENESIS & A BRIEF HISTORY

My father was the Oyokohene of Kumasi and when my sister (Agnes Addo Kufuor) got married to the reigning and British-knighted Asantehene (the late Sir Osei Tutu Agyeman Prempeh II) that path to the Manhyia Palace was even easier to travail. It meant that my nephew—Kyeretwie Prempeh—consolidated the familial ties. A framework, therefore, existed to know Kyerematen better. Kyeretwie Prempeh, who had attended a public school in England and would later enter the School of Oriental and African Studies (SOAS) of University of London in London, took the path of his mentor, Kyerematen. He would however be recalled home to Kumasi, the Ashanti regional capital, to take up leadership of the family Stool of Apagya. Very young and following family call for responsibility, Dr. Kyerematen adopted him, indeed with the intention of grooming him to take over the future directorship of the then Asante Cultural Centre (which is now the famous Ghana National Cultural Centre). However, this was not to be, as Kyeretwie Prempeh became a chief "forever" until he died.

As I vividly recall, it was when I returned home to Kumasi from Exeter College of the University of Oxford in 1966, as a young lawyer, that I got to know Dr. Kyerematen better. He had by then left the Office of the Town Clerk of Kumasi to take up full-time work at the re-named Ghana National Cultural Centre. I was in my mid-20s, and I was interested in politics as well as in public service. He encouraged me in my interests, and I was eventually made the Town Clerk, his earlier position.

The overthrow of the Nkrumah Government in 1966—coupled with the subsequent return from exile of Professor Kofi Abrefa ("K.A.") Busia, the arch opponent of deposed President Nkrumah—intensified my interest in the partisan politics of Ghana; my respect for Dr. Busia was for many reasons, including his serious scholarship, which included his important two books on education, *Purposeful Education for Africa* (1964) as well as the one on democracy, *Africa In Search of Democracy* (1967). Dr. Kyerematen was also interested in politics generally; yet, with the background that he had, he would not be the soap-box type or a platform one; instead, he intended to use the power of politics for cultural development of Ghanaian society. He had been made Commissioner for Local Government under the National Liberation Council (NLC), after the 1966 coup but that was basically for development but not partisan purposes.

When I intimated to Dr. Kyerematen my own interest in going into Ghana's Parliament and, therefore, to contest the constituency primary of the United Party-Progress Party in 1968, he (Kyerematen) encouraged me. From varied sources, I also heard, while serving as the Town Clerk of Kumasi, that he (Dr. Kyerematen) wanted to represent Kumasi in the 1968 Constituent Assembly to help in drafting a new constitution for Ghana. I, therefore, out of respect for Dr. Kyerematen agreed to stand aside, although it would also have been a formidable attempt for me; that was why I, instead, left Kumasi area alone in order to contest a seat in the rural district of Atwima Nwabiagya Constituency, also in the Ashanti Region. I was successful, and that eventually became the base of my parliamentary career.

Indeed, the centenary of Dr. Kyerematen's birth passed with a mild remembrance, as his family wanted it to be. Furthermore, it was also very much in accordance with the patriarch's modest nature. However, his deeds in cultural awareness that are being passed on to generations today and those yet to be born, certainly a century after his birth, tell very much in themselves.

I am very happy to point out unequivocally in this Foreword that the foundations of Ghana's cultural landscape are stronger today, in part, due to the hard work of an African cultural hero like Dr. Kyerematen. If the past lives in the present and with us, the book—thematically styling him as West *African Cultural Prince*—that has beautifully been dedicated by the co-authors to his very devoted widow (Mrs. Victoria Kyerematen) and late daughter (Mrs. Kyerematen-Darko), will go a long way to affirm Dr. Kyerematen as the true doyen of Ghana's cultural advancement, thereby making the blessed centenarian rest in perfect peace!

His Excellency John Agyekum Kufuor
Former President of the Republic of Ghana (2001–2009)
Chairman of John Agyekum Kufuor Foundation,
Aburi, Eastern Region, Ghana

Preface

Soon after the British colonial Gold Coast attained statehood on 6th March, 1957 as independent Ghana, Prof. J. H. Kwabena Nkekia (1921–2019), a distinguished Ethnomusicologist, was credited with fashioning an initial national Cultural Policy document for political leaders of the new Ghana, led by the first indigenous Prime Minister Kwame Nkrumah (1909–1972). While that document did not spark the beginning of Ghana's cultural awareness; it was still deemed an important recognition of the new nation's either regional or geographic leadership in highlighting the beauty and diversity of culture in the former Gold Coast, which became a British crown colony from March 6, 1821 until March 6, 1957. (Assensoh & Alex-Assensoh, 2022; Arhin, 1991; Assensoh, 1998). Indeed, the cultural policy document that Dr. Nketia drafted for Ghana was so crucial for the new country and its West African neighbors that UNESCO and, since then, successive Ghanaian governments have used it as a reference point.

While the Nkrumah government's policy making ambiance set the framework for cultural preservation, it also took a clear-cut vision, hands and feet, *per se*, to do the work needed to build centers and other structures that could host cultural assets, and subsequently to continue to foster cultural awareness and eventual revival. In the foregoing context, drum majors, for culture, were acutely necessary as well as vital, and that was where Dr. A.A.Y. Kyerematen did come into play—as a leading drum major for culture in Ghana and, by extension, across West Africa and, indeed, throughout the continent of Africa.

That is why almost four decades after the death of Dr. Kyerematen, Ghana is still known to be a citadel for rich indigenous culture, so much so that in 2019, the political leaders of Ghana, with cultural awareness in vogue, launched the widely celebrated "Year of Return, 1619–2019," an invitation to continental Africans as well as diaspora-based Africans in the United States of America, the Caribbean and, most certainly, around the world to return to Ghana to celebrate their cultural roots. With much success and fanfare, Ghana welcomed thousands of Africans from around the world, who traveled to the former slave-shipping Gold Coast—now Ghana since 1957—to explore their culture in ways that would have been impossible, if not for the hard work and visionary leadership of Dr. Kyerematen, who, in turn, built on a keen understanding of Ghana's important role in documenting and showcasing its cultural history, indeed with the support of the visionary indigenous leader (Nkrumah) and other nationalist pioneers often labelled as the Big Six. (Assensoh, 1998; Arhin, 1991; Assensoh and Alex-Assensoh, 2022).

The foregoing crucial historical-*cum*-cultural factors are among the top reasons why we felt deeply honored, when a member of the distinguished family of the late Dr. Kyerematen of Kumasi, Ghana, agreed with the suggestion to complete this publication in honor of his memory and legacy. Indeed, Dr. Kyerematen, the founding director of the Kumasi-based Ghana National Cultural Centre, upon his death in 1976, left a distinguished memory and, most certainly, a viable cultural legacy that should be cherished by all and sundry. His life reminds all, who knew him very well, of the Ghana Akan proverb, "It is not until the frog dies that you know how long it is."

Indeed, the impact of Dr. Kyerematen's cultural work, within the context of his cultural anthropological discipline, is far reaching, most certainly beyond what his modest demeanor would suggest. Indeed, when people throughout the world think about distinctive culture on the continent of Africa, the nation of Ghana, as a citadel and purveyor of rich indigenous culture, is high on the list. That standing is due, in no small part, to the quiet but effective foundation that Dr. Kyerematen laid prior to and also during Ghana's early post-colonial days. In writing this book, the Assensohs hope to cast light on the foundation that he laid for Ghana, Africa and beyond in order to illuminate the tremendous cultural resources and assets of the country and the continent.

Indeed, in the slim mini-biography, titled *30 Years Into Eternity*, readers are informed by the Editor about how it "dawned on him [Dr. Kyerematen] that there was the urgent need for the preservation of our rich cultural heritage, not only in writing but, in such concrete forms as museums, zoos, craft centers for indigenous Ghanaian Craftsmen and traditional music and dancing" (Editor, 2006, p. 11). Furthermore, Dr. Kyerematen's plans, as quoted by the editor, included the following: The rest are drama troupes, archives, theaters as well as a library, where books about [African] arts and culture could be made readily available for aspiring Ghanaians (and any other nationals, who are interested in culture) wanting to learn or research more into them. He envisioned the difficulties ahead and faced them squarely drawing a comprehensive program of activities to realize his dream. (Editor, 2006, p. 13)

While formulating all of the foregoing plans, he was also dreaming about his future scholarship, which included returning to the United Kingdom for his doctoral degree at the University of Cambridge's King's College. Dr. Kyerematen knew that the advanced degree and the writing of his doctoral dissertation would be a tremendous asset. So in preparing for the Cambridge program, he agreed to serve as the secretary to the Asante Confederacy Council, which thereafter decided to shed the word "Confederacy" from the name, as it simply became the Asanteman Council in 1952.

Although Dr. Kyerematen had the inclination for further studies in order to brighten his future in scholarly pursuits, he also decided to utilize the opportunity of working for the council, which was headed by the Asantehene, Otumfuo Sir Osei Agyeman Prempeh II, to seek assistance in acquiring the requisite land to start work on the Asante Cultural Centre, as was its initial name. In the words of the editor of *30 Years into Eternity*: "Nana Prempeh supported the idea, and not only did His majesty provide him with land, but also assisted financially to enable him to implement this laudable dream of his," (Editor, *op* cit, p. 13). To emphasize the region's rich assets, Dr. Kyerematen envisioned the Centre to include "a model cocoa farm indicating agriculture as the main pre-occupation of the farmers of this great nation of ours. Thus, any tourist visiting the [centre] could have a feel of our rural life, which depicts most of our customs, tradition and culture," (Editor, pp. 13–15).

This book offers a fuller understanding of the vision, context, and legacy of Dr. Kyerematen, and it is divided into three sections in order to provide an easy roadmap for the readers to follow as well as to edify: (I) Foundations; (II) Building; and (III) Legacy.

Section I, Foundations focuses on what made Dr. Kyerematen who he was—family, culture and education. Section II, Building, does explore the crucial active planning as well as actual building process for the Centre, coupled with the partisan as well as cultural politics that he had to negotiate for it to exist and also to thrive till this day. Section III, Legacy, focuses on his enviable legacy of service, the continuing impact of his work through his surviving widow as well as his children, and the ongoing impact today of his cultural overall legacy nationally (in Ghana), regionally (in West Africa), and continentally (in Africa).

Ivor Agyeman-Duah

Acknowledgments

In completing this publication, we owe unlimited debts of gratitude to several people, the foremost of which are the members of Dr. A. A. Y. Kyerematen's nuclear family, made up of his devoted widow, Lady Victoria Kyerematen (*nee* Welsing), his wonderful children and several extended family members (already referenced by name in various parts of the publication).

Most certainly, we cannot thank enough His Excellency John Agyekum Kufuor, the very popular two-term President of Ghana (2001–2009), who took a look at a draft of our manuscript and, with a Lawyer's keen eyes, agreed to provide the Foreword to this book with no hesitation. We learned from discussions with former President Kufuor, who is popularly described by his admirers as a "gentle giant," that he takes a sagacious view of the supremacy of culture in Ghana. Most certainly, we are eternally grateful to him, given his very closeness to Dr. Kyerematen of blessed memory.

In a folkloric remembrance, Ex-President Kufuor pointed out unabashedly, in our brief but very meaningful discussions with him, that Dr. Kyerematen was known to have eschewed partisan politics in a variety of ways. Yet, he (former President Kufuor) felt that the cultural prince of Africa (Dr. Kyerematen) had a very astute political acumen because of the very prescient piece of advice he offered him when he (as a young Lawyer) was thinking about entering partisan politics without easily thinking of possible pitfalls. At the time, then Lawyer Kufuor, as a result, was interested in choosing between Atwima Nwabiagya Constituency, outside the Ashanti regional capital (Kumasi) and the Subin Constituency, Kumasi, to run for his initial parliamentary electoral contest.

"Dr. Kyerematen suggested the Atwima Nwabiagya Constituency as a much smaller as well as a lot more manageable and also safer constituency than Subin. I accepted his advice; handily, I won the parliamentary seat, and that successfully launched me into Progress Party (P.P.) politics, with Professor K.A. Busia as the national Flag Bearer," future President Kufuor disclosed. Consequently, it was very crucial that Ex-President Kufuor agreed to write the Foreword to this book; and we are eternally grateful to him.

We are also grateful to University of Oregon School of Law's retired Nash Law Professor Ibrahim Gassama, who promptly agreed to write the Introduction, which has turned out—in the description of earlier proofreaders and by our own assessment as co-authors—to be an insightful contribution to this publication. We are also very grateful to his dear wife, whom we refer affectionately to as Sister Marva Gassama (*née* Solomon), and their dear beloved daughter, Fatima—Iowa-based doctoral student—for being patient when Professor Gassama was researching to complete the very meaningful Introduction that he has generously contributed. The great Kyerematen family of Ghana has teamed up with us in expressing our eternal gratitude to the Gassama family of Eugene, Oregon (now in Chicago, Illinois).

Furthermore, for various reasons, we are very grateful to Ghana's distinguished writer and well-known author of several notable books, Ivor Agyeman-Duah; as a writer and a Development Specialist, he has written extensively on varied topical subjects, including economics, international development as well as cooperation and literary histories. Apart from readily agreeing to write the preface to this publication, he is known also to be an Adviser to former Ghana President John Agyekum Kufuor, an Oxford-educated Lawyer, as well as an Adviser to Ashanti King Osei Tutu II during his historic visit to the Seychelles, of which Adviser Ivor Agyeman-Duah produced two televised documentaries, titled *Yaa Asante Waa: The Heroism of an African Queen*, and *The Return of a King to Seychelles*. Known for his hard work as a former Ghana diplomat and also as a prolific author, he was part of the BBC and PBS production team for *Wonders of the African World*, which was presented by Distinguished Professor Henry Louis Gates, Jr. of Harvard University.

We are very grateful to Anthropologist Peter Akwasi Pipim, a retired employee of the Smithsonian Institution, Washington, DC, who played a mini-fatherly roll for the Kyerematen children when their famous father was very busy with the work of his Kumasi-based center; as well as University of Oxford-educated late Dr. Alex Quaison-Sackey (1924–1992), Ghana's former famous Ambassador to the United Nations from 1959 to 1965 and also, briefly, Ghana's Foreign Minister from 1965 to 1966; and Emeritus Catholic Archbishop Peter Akwasi Sarpong, (born on 6th February 1933), all of whom were kind enough to be interviewed for the book. We are similarly grateful to several Librarians in Oregon working for Eugene Public Library and also at University of Oregon, who combined their expertise to help us to access some of Dr. Kyerematen's available published works, including his University of Cambridge's King's College dissertation that we received for temporary research use through inter-library loaning system.

Additionally, we are very grateful to Livingston Alex Kwabena Assensoh, creative director of L.A.C.E-Hearted LLC, who helped to select map/tabular and photo illustrations for the book and, most certainly, Kwadwo Stephen Alex Assensoh, a former Research Analyst at University of Oregon, who spent some quality time to comb through the manuscript and, as part of the preparation process as well as offering valuable suggestions on how the manuscript could be strengthened in a variety of ways. Kwadwo was there in Ghana when we interviewed some of our selected subjects. Also, we are eternally grateful to Special Assistant to the Vice President for Equity and Inclusion, Lady Tracy Bars as well as Dr. Augustine Adu Frimpong of Southern University and A&M College of Louisiana, both of whom generously assisted us in making sure of the proper formatting of the manuscript. We thank both of them and their respective families most sincerely!

We, as well, owe special debts of gratitude to Dr. Gabriel ("Agya") Kyerematen, a well-known Medical Practitioner in the USA, and his late sister, Mrs. Bridget Kyerematen-Darko (one of the two family members to whom the book is dedicated). Their active encouragement and support made possible the initial trip to Ghana for interviews for the book, indeed dating back to 2017. Above all, we are very grateful to the various publishers of Dr. Kyerematen's publications, on which we have partially relied as we researched and completed the manuscript for this book. We owe a debt of gratitude to all such publishers—including Longmans, Green & Company of the United Kingdom—as well as Dr. Kyerematen's nuclear family members for sharing several pieces of rich information and pictorial illustrations with us, some of which are to appear in this book. We have in mind other family members: Lawyer Alan Kwadwo Kyerematen, a former Ghana cabinet member; Nana Osei Kyerematen, a retired Insurance Corporate Leader; Rev. Richard Kyerematen of Pennsylvania; and Maame Serwaa Kyerematen, a Howard University-educated (MFA) Fine Arts' professional.

We are grateful for some specific institutional information utilized for illustrative purposes only, indeed, to share with readers information about some of the prestigious educational institutions that Dr. Kyerematen attended, including Fourah Bay College (Sierra Leone), West Africa as well as Durham University; University of Oxford; and Cambridge University, all in the United Kingdom. Above all, we are grateful to individuals, who shared brief conversations with us about Dr. Kyerematen but, being so long ago, their names have escaped our memory; yet, we are grateful to all.

This book is published today because Hamilton Books' Associate Editor Brooke Bures and Assistant Production Editor Rachel Hungerford believed in us; therefore, in collaboration with Lexington Books' Acquisition Editor Sydney Wedbush, they secured a book contract for our work. We are eternally grateful to them and their hard-working office staff employees.

Introduction

Fourah Bay College, Sierra Leone, in the Context of the Life and Times Of Dr. A. A. Y. Kyerematen of Ghana

I deem it very auspicious in contributing this Introduction to *Africa's Cultural Prince: Dr. A.A.Y. Kyerematen of Ghana*, a very timely biography of one of West Africa's very significant intellectual figures. Indeed, as youngsters in Sierra Leonean secondary schools—which were the equivalent of American high schools—our educational ambitions included the fact that one day, with the requisite entrance qualifications, including the then advanced level certificates of University of London's General Certificate of Education (G.C.E.), we would emulate the intellectual examples of Dr. Kyerematen of Ghana and others. Therefore, we had plans, foremost, to attend Fourah Bay College, one of the Ghanaian scholar's *alma maters*.

Even, as young as we were, we knew that the college was, indeed, the oldest higher educational institution, with university status, in the West Africa sub-region. Furthermore, we were very much aware of the fact that Fourah Bay College had an arranged affiliation with such a British higher educational institution as Durham University in Durham, which is in northeast England.

Several of us, as school-going young boys and girls, lived in the suburbs of Freetown, the national capital. At the time, we knew that Fourah Bay College—now a constituent institution of the University of Sierra Leone—was one of the major institutions of higher learning that, one day, we will attend. Therefore, we liked to visit its campus in the Mount Aureol neighborhood of the national capital. After all, we had our own aspirations of attending these local universities and teacher training colleges in the future. We did not, at the time, know that some of us would travel overseas for further studies, as I did, for example.

However, what motivated several of us to dream of attending Fourah Bay College—which was attended by Dr. A. A. Y. Kyerematen of Ghana—was that we were also aware that our well-educated countrymen and country-women studied there with other citizens from Dr. Kyerematen's Ghana as well as other neighboring countries like the Republics of The Gambia, Liberia, Nigeria and Côte d'Ivoire (Ivory Coast), who travelled to Sierra Leone to attend Fourah Bay College.

Consequently, I was not surprised to learn that non-Sierra-Leonian scholars and, indeed, my former University of Oregon colleagues (Professors A. B. Assensoh and Yvette M. Alex-Assensoh) were writing about Dr. Kyerematen, the founder and the first famous Director of the Kumasi-based Ghana National Cultural Center. After attending Fourah Bay College, as earlier mentioned, the future Dr. Kyerematen continued his education at Durham University, followed by his successful stints at Oxford and Cambridge Universities, also in the United Kingdom. Most certainly, the Ghana-born Anthropologist was out, at the time, in search of the proverbial golden fleece.

On our part, as youngsters from West Africa, several of us had different higher education trajectories. Therefore, seizing the opportunity on my part, for example, to attend Virginia Tech University in Blacksburg and, later, Harvard University School of Law, both in the United States, I forfeited my chance to follow illustrious Africans like Dr. Kyerematen to pursue academic degree studies at Fourah Bay College.

In spite of the missed opportunity, I still have the highest respect and admiration for youngsters of my age and those before us, at the time, who chose to stay home in Sierra Leone to attend Fourah Bay College. As I still recall, I very much remember reading about the college, as a teenager, and learning in the process that, like all other universities, it had what the British-style system refer to as faculties of arts, social sciences as well as of pure and applied sciences, coupled with professional schools specializing in both engineering and law.

Apart from the obvious British colonial educational connection with Fourah Bay College, we also knew that the Anglican Church, known in the United Kingdom as the Church of England, had a hand in establishing the institution, which historically dates back to February 1827. We were very much aware that many of the college's administrative leaders were foreigners, mostly from the United Kingdom. However, we were proud to learn later that, by 1966, the first Sierra Leonean to head Fourah Bay College was Dr. Davidson Abioseh Nicol (1924–1994), who was a Cambridge University-trained medical doctor, but he chose to serve in various administrative positions in and outside of his beloved Sierra Leone. Among places he served, with distinction, was the United Nations in New York.

Interestingly, when I moved to the United States, I was very happy to learn from my older siblings that Fourah Bay College's former head (Dr. Nicol), indeed, occupied very important positions at the United Nations, including being Director of the United Nations' Institute for Training and Research (UNITAR). When eventually the U.N. had its first African secretary-general, Egypt's Boutros Boutros-Ghali, followed immediately by Ghana's Kofi Annan as the second African head of the United Nations, I was not surprised to learn that, in fact, the U.N. had always had African men and women diplomats playing leadership roles. For example, the first African woman to serve as president of the U.N. General Assembly was Liberia's then U.N. ambassador, Angie Brooks-Randolph, who later became her country's first female Supreme Court Justice on May 6, 1977.

Ghana's distinguished diplomat, Dr. Alex Quaison-Sackey, was also an earlier African president of the United Nations' General Assembly, when he served the late President Kwame Nkrumah's Convention People's Party (CPP) government as its Ambassador and Plenipotentiary to the United Nations.

As shown from the catalogue of successes on the part of various Africans, their remarkable achievements as diplomats, professionals and otherwise were commensurate with their education and qualifications. Small wonder then, indeed, that after his Fourah Bay and Durham University education, Dr. Kyerematen returned to the then Gold Coast to carve a stellar niche for himself by establishing the country's National Cultural Centre. After independence on March 6, 1957, from Britain, the Gold Coast was re-named Ghana, in fact after one of the four names of the empires that preceded colonialism, (i.e., Ghana, Guinea, Mali and Songhay).

My good friends and co-authors of this marvelous publication (the Assensohs) have noted in their well-researched work that in 1962, the first indigenous head of state of Ghana (the late President Kwame Nkrumah) visited Kumasi, where the center—at the time known as Asante Cultural Centre—was based. The center, which soon gained national prominence, was offered instant official recognition as well as the financial support by Dr. Nkrumah's government for Dr. Kyerematen's hard work. Therefore, it was re-named Ghana's National Cultural Centre. The Ghanaian leader at the time (Dr. Nkrumah) had himself studied in the United States and—like Dr. Kyerematen—also in the United Kingdom at the London School of Economics. Therefore, he saw how selfless Dr. Kyerematen had been by utilizing his education and knowledge in the interests of his Ashanti ethnic group and also as a patriotic citizen of Ghana. These were, as a result, the sole reasons that prompted then President Nkrumah to provide national assistance to Dr. Kyerematen's center because of its cultural value for the country but, certainly, not for partisan political reasons.

Most certainly, with this humble introduction to this book, I am very happy to be identified or associated with the noble name of Dr. Kyerematen, whose centennial birth year was 2016. Apart from this publication planned in honor of Dr. Kyerematen's 100th birthday, the family at home and abroad, on the auspicious occasion, had their noble plans to remember their late distinguished patriarch in such a formal manner. It was hoped that officials of Fourah Bay College would also be informed of this important occasion in order for them to remember the centennial birthday of their worthy alumnus. In that way Fourah Bay College's current leaders—including some of my former Sierra Leonean classmates—may be in a position to show and also to celebrate their own appreciation for the noble Pan-Africanist deeds of Dr. Kyerematen back in Ghana. After all, what Dr. Kyerematen did in Ghana, with the founding of the Centre to promote African culture in general but Ghanaian culture in particular, fell within the purview of the Pan-Africanist ideals preached loudly by Ghana's late President Nkrumah as well as the legendary Dr. W. E. B. DuBois, George Padmore, Kenyan President Jomo Kenyatta, Tanzanian President Julius K. Nyerere, Dr. C. L. R. James of Trinidad and Tobago and other deceased, dedicated Pan-Africanists.

DR. KYEREMATEN'S VIABLE
LEGACY IN WEST AFRICA

From conversations and also culled from available pieces of written information, it is very remarkable to learn that Dr. Kyerematen's cultural impact extends beyond his home country. For, the cultural awareness that the Ghanaian cultural hero instituted in Ghana (when it was still called the Gold Coast) through his Ghana National Cultural Centre is now being impacted throughout West Africa. The reason stems from the formation on May 28, 1975 of the Economic Community of West African States (ECOWAS), which is known in French as CEDEAO. As a result of this political and economic union of all of West African nations and their estimated population of not less than 340 million citizens, most nations in the region have come to know about Dr. Kyerematen's noble deeds for Ghana, thus the establishment of the Ghana National Cultural Center, and its genesis through its national hero.

As more and more West Africans now have travel privileges to visit ECOWAS nations without visa requirement (in fact, with the green ECOWAS passport), it has become a lot easier for the citizens to move around the sub-region. When its common currency is introduced, trade and other financial activities will easily be streamlined. As travel has become so easy, whenever ECOWAS citizens from the other African nations visit Ghana, places and institutions they are encouraged to visit include the Kumasi-based

Ghana National Cultural Center, which was conceived and established by Dr. Kyerematen. Other African citizens, visiting the Center have returned to their nations on the continent –particularly in West Africa—to agitate for the establishment of a similar cultural institution. Due to that, Dr. Kyerematen's name has become a household word and, indeed, is part of the reasons I feel very strongly that this book, about his life and times, can very easily be adopted as a textbook in several African countries.

As I conclude my brief, but very purposeful introduction to this fine biographical study of Dr. Kyerematen of blessed memory, I wish to memorialize him as the Ghanaian cultural hero, who is aptly described in this book as a cultural prince of Africa.

Ibrahim Gassama
University of Oregon School of Law (Emeritus)

Chapter 1

Dr. Kyerematen's Birth, Educational Pursuits and Intellectual Growth

When Dr. Kyerematen was born on 29th April, 1916, to Mr. Emmanuel Kwasi Dwira Kyerematen of Bompata and his wife, Madam Rebecca Boatin (*née* Madam Akosua Dwimoh) of the Patasi royal family, in the Ashanti Region of Ghana, he was given the full name of Alexander Atta Yaw Kyerematen. He was the grandson of Nana Kwame Boatin, Kyidomhene of Kumasi from 1896 to 1923. Today, the surname of the mother will be spelled as Boateng. His second name, Atta, should have signified that he was born a male twin, but he was not.

In fact, over the years, his name was abbreviated as Dr. A. A. Y. Kyerematen, both for convenience and also to accommodate the many foreign dignitaries he encountered in his lifetime, including his former European professors, classmates and other foreign friends in the United Kingdom and elsewhere. Apart from finding the abbreviations fanciful at times, it must be said that several foreign teachers, associates, friends and colleagues claim that they often find several long African names intimidating; hence some Africans choose to abbreviate their names to accommodate them.

While young Atta Kyerematen's father originally came from Bompata, which is in the Asante Akim area and about 20 miles away from the Ashanti regional capital of Kumasi, where he worked, his mother hailed from the royal family of Patasi, a suburb of Kumasi. The father's move to Kumasi was due to his innovative business position, which earned him the nickname or accolade of "Broker King" ("Broker Hene") of Kumasi. In later years, as an adult, Dr. Kyerematen's uncle—who occupied the chieftaincy position at Patasi (as the *Odikro*) passed away, so he was consequently installed as the new chief (*Odikro*) of the town, in keeping with Ashanti custom, which bestows royalty or inheritance through matriarchal lineage. This was

7

a lifetime position occupied by Dr. Kyerematen until he passed away in 1976. In fact, through maternal inheritance, he could have also inherited the Kyidomhene of Kumasi traditional title since he was the grandson of the late Kyidomhene.

Dr. Kyeromaten, by circumstances of birth and heritage, was born into the Ashanti ethnic group, which in the British colonial era was considered to be one of the major tribal or ethnic kingdoms in West Africa. He was born into the Patase royal family because of his mother, as the Ashantis inherit through one's matrilineal line of birth, just like the British. When growing up in the Ashanti Region of the Gold Coast, which was renamed Ghana on Independence Day on March 6, 1957, an Ashanti King (or *Asantehene*) that Dr. Kyerematen happened to know well and eventually to befriend was Otumfuo Sir Nana Osei Tutu Agyeman Prempeh II, who was respected so much by the British colonial authorities that he was knighted as Knight of the British Empire (KBE).

According to Ashanti royal historical archives, King (*Asantehene*) Prempeh II was born in the year 1892 in Kumasi, the regional capital. He was barely four years old when, as the Crown Prince of the Ashanti Royal Family, his family members—including the 13th King (or *Asantehene*), Prempeh I— were considered so "stubborn" that they were arrested by the British colonial authorities (who took over the Gold Coast on March 6, 1844 through the so-called "Bond of 1844") and exiled to the Seychelles Islands in 1896. Among other royal family members also exiled with the King were the young Crown Prince's maternal grandmother (Ashanti Queen Nana Yaa Akyaa) and several selective royal family members. An arrangement was made later to allow Prempeh I to return to Kumasi, but as *Kumasihene* (Chief of Kumasi) but not as *Asantehene* (King); the return took place or was effected in 1924, but he lived only seven more years, as he died of natural causes in 1931.

Through British colonial intrigues, the young Crown Prince was not allowed to become the next (14th) King of the Ashanti people (or the *Asantehene*). Instead, he succeeded Prempeh I as the *Kumasihene* upon his death. With assurances and reassurances of healthy or cordial collaboration with the British colonial authorities, he was installed (or enstooled) as the new King (*Asantehene*) on June 22, 1931, which meant that when he died on May 27, 1970, he had reigned for a long time.

As will be seen in the second section of the book, the relationship between Kyerematen and the Asantehene deepened so much that, at one time, Dr. Kyerematen, as a young man, served as the Secretary of the Ashanti Traditional Council, headed by the King. That relationship was important for the acquisition of land on which the Center was established.

EDUCATIONAL BACKGROUND

Since education plays an important role in the lives of young men and women in former colonial countries, young Kyerematen understood the importance of getting a good education. Therefore, he started his elementary school education at the then Government Boys School in Kumasi, where he was selected to serve as the senior prefect (senior pupil) by his teachers and classmates. Academically, he showed an avowed interest in the study of history, which was in future to influence his choice of academic pursuits and profession. Upon the completion of his elementary school education at the middle school level, he sat for and passed with flying colors the relevant national common entrance examination at the age of 16 to enter Adisadel College in Cape Coast in 1932.

Earning General Certificate Of Education

Young Kyerematen was known to be very studious, winning several of the available prizes and awards of Adisadel College, which included the prestigious Dyce-Sharp Essay Prize, accolades which prompted the institutions' leaders in the mid-1930s to insert Kyerematen's name on Adisadel College's "Board of Honours." He was listed as the best scholar in English for two consecutive years, in 1935 and in 1936. At that time, brilliant students were selected for certain earmarked professions and admitted to prestigious institutions of further learning.

Religious Life at Adisadel College:
Interesting Developments

The religious life of the Adisadel College, during the years of the future Dr. Kyerematen, as some interviewees narrated, was taken good care of. Attendance at Church services on Sundays was compulsory. A large hall at Topp Yard was converted into a Chapel, where the boys worshipped on Sundays and mass was said daily in the morning before school began for the day. This saved the boys the trouble of walking to and from Christ Church some distance away for the purpose. Indeed, the College's Chapel was the first to use The English Hymnal in place of the standard *Hymns: Ancient and Modern* which has been in use in all the Churches of the Diocese for many years. It was also the place where the solemn ceremony of "Blessing the Sixth Formers" and "Induction of the Head Prefect" into office, both instituted by Father Knight himself, were first held in the presence of a large congregation, including parents and guardians of the boys.

The classical fervor of the College reached its zenith with the staging of impressive Greek plays. The first, *Antigone*, staged in 1934–1935 was intended to mark the School's Silver Jubilee, which was celebrated with great pomp in 1935. The play was well received by the public. By popular requests, there was a repeat performance before a full house at Cape Coast. It was later staged at Sekondi and then moved to Kumasi. The theatrical scenery and the costume of the cast as well as their histrionics contributed much to its success. Of course, the success was to the credit of Stephen Nicholas, who planned, selected the cast of actors and produced the play. Perhaps, his familiarity with plays and drama was refined and enhanced at Adisadel, and laid the foundation for how Kyerematen incorporated the arts into his cultural work at the Centre.

Studying Religion and Sacred Ministry

That was why young Kyerematen, upon completing Adisadel College scoring merit (including what was known as the University of Oxford's Responsions) in the final external examinations, the headmaster of Adisadel College recommended that he train for what was then known as sacred ministry (the priesthood) at Trinity College, near University of the Gold Coast (now University of Ghana). So, between 1937 and 1939, young Kyerematen trained to become an Anglican priest. However, before ordination, he was offered a scholarship to study at Fourah Bay College in Sierra Leone.

Earning Inter B.A. Status in History

In a diary that Dr. Kyerematen kept religiously to record important happenings, he had inscribed how he transferred from Fourah Bay College in Sierra Leone, a West Africa-based constituent college of University of Durham in the United Kingdom, in order to complete his requirement for a full-fledged bachelor art (B.A.) degree in history, with a second-class (Upper Division) accolade. In fact, from the available records, including letters of recommendation from his tutors and professors, he missed a first-class division degree by a few points (or marks, as they are known in the British educational system). Kyerematen started degree studies at Fourah Bay College in Freetown, Sierra Leone. His seemingly easy entry was due to excellent final school certificate results at Adisadel College, as explained above.

The young Kyerematen took time to do his homework very well about the Sierra Leone-based institution, as he noted in one of the early diaries he fondly kept that he liked what he read about Fourah Bay College. Since he also planned to study in the United Kingdom, the young man was delighted that the institution had a strong British affiliation. Eventually, Alexander

Atta Yaw Kyerematen chose to study and earn advanced (postgraduate) degrees from the Universities of Oxford and Cambridge, respectively. Fourah Bay College (later University of Sierra Leone) had academic leaders of distinction, who worked hard to mold young minds, including that of Dr. Kyerematen. For example, most of the early principals of Fourah Bay College were Caucasian expatriates, who had earned British educational credentials. Among the first black Principals of the university was Rev. Edward Jones, an African American from South Carolina. Among the early local academic employees was Lamina Sankoh.

Then, the late Cambridge University-educated Dr. Davidson Abioseh Nicol, in 1966, became the first Sierra Leonean to serve as Principal of Fourah Bay College. From there, he embraced the service of the United Nations as under-secretary general as well as the executive director of the United Nations Institute for Training and Research (UNITAR).

Fourah Bay College, which the young Kyerematen attended between 1939 and 1941, had an affiliation with the United Kingdom-based Durham University. Therefore, for the young Kyerematen to earn his history degree, he was required to travel to the United Kingdom to enroll at Durham. That desire became a possibility in 1946, when the Asanteman Council awarded him a merit scholarship to 30-year-old Kyerematen for further studies, with which he studied and earned his bachelor of arts degree in history, with distinction from Durham. While there, he was a noted athlete. Upon his return to the then Gold Coast, he briefly taught in local schools until 1946 when he made up his mind to leave for the United Kingdom to continue his studies, with the interest to enroll in postgraduate studies in history.

Earning A B. Litt Anthropology Degree

Subsequently, young Kyerematen earned his postgraduate bachelor of letters (B.Litt.) degree in anthropology from Keble College of University of Oxford. It is very coincidental that the young Kyerematen, who initially studied theology but left at the end to go to Fourah Bay College to study history, would later enroll at an Oxford college, where several theologians were educated. Therefore, the institution was characteristically designed as an all-male institution. Having studied in the United Kingdom, Dr. Kyerematen had several contemporaries from Ghana and other African countries, who followed similar educational plans to study and earn academic and professional degrees from the mother country of several colonial nations. Interestingly, however, several of such ambitious youngsters were much younger than he was, but they did later on in their professional pursuits find the time as well as the interests to know, admire and, in some cases, support Dr. Kyerematen's interests in establishing what later became as the Ghana National Cultural Centre in Kumasi, which served as the capital of Ghana's Ashanti Region.

Interestingly, it his study at Oxford University, one of the most learned universities in the world with its limited understanding of Ghanaian culture in particular and African culture, more broadly, that convinced him of the need to return home and establish a regime of processes and programs to enhance the understanding of Ghanaian culture in Ghana and abroad. And the rest, as they say, is history.

Earning a Doctor Of Philosophy (D Phil. in Anthropology)

It was in 1965 that Dr. Kyerematen returned to King's College, University of Cambridge, where he had secured admission to complete his doctoral degree. The Asanteman Council had assisted him financially to pursue his earlier studies. This time he competed for a scholarship of the International African Institute (IAI) to complete his studies. By accepting this scholarship award, Dr. Kyerematen had to offer the IAI the first option of publishing the research that would culminate in a dissertation. The topic of his dissertation was: "Ashanti Royal Regalia: An Ethno-History of Ashanti Kingship."

Dr. Kyerematen operated in a multi-faceted way, pursuing his Cambridge studies while still developing the cultural centre idea, a fact perfectly captured in a statement made by Dr. Evans Anfom, himself a leading academician and scholar, who served for several years as the vice-chancellor of the Kwame Nkrumah University of Science and Technology (KNUST), on whose council Dr. Kyerematen ably served and then even chaired for some time. Dr. Anfom, who later became the chairman of the West African Examinations Council (WAEC), saw Dr. Kyerematen as a crusader, who was assisted by a handful of similar-minded and very capable people. He was quoted by an editor as saying: "The spade work and the moving spirit behind every successful development always involves just a handful of selfless and devoted individuals, who are very often born before their age" (p. 7). In the chapter that follows, we provide detailed information on the institutions, which would mold Dr. Kyerematen into a formidable scholar, including King's College of Cambridge University, where Dr. Kyerematen chose in 1965 to become a *bona fide* holder of a doctorate, attaining the accolades that several of his scholarly colleagues and friends had acquired. Fellow scholars—like Dr. Evans Anform and others, who were not only friends of his, but also worked with him on academic campuses—opined that he was so brilliant and ready for postgraduate studies that he could have done his doctoral studies anywhere in Europe or the United States of America.

Chapter 2

Dr. Kyerematen's Higher Learning

In the end, when Dr. Alexander Atta Yaw Kyerematen returned from his quest for academic laurels to settle down in his native Gold Coast—which was the natural-resource enriched British colony that changed its name to Ghana at independence on March 6, 1957—he could boast of education from such prestigious British academic institutions of higher learning as University of Durham, University of Oxford's Keble College, and, finally, King's College of Cambridge University. These foundations provided the basis for building process that we discuss later.

It was, indeed, very important for the future Dr. Kyerematen to share with family members, friends, and professional colleagues the stature of the institutions he attended, as he noted in his diary. From several notes he kept, we have been able to provide readers of this book with information about the various universities he attended, something that his late daughter, Mrs. Bridget Kyerematen-Darko, indicated to us that her dear father would have liked to showcase in either a memoir or an autobiography, if he had completed one like Ghana's first elected indigenous leader, the late Osagyefo President Kwame Nkrumah, whose autobiography was published to coincide with Ghana's independence in 1957.

At the dawn of Ghana's independence that year (on March 6th), Nkrumah's life story was showcased in *Ghana: Autobiography of Kwame Nkrumah*, which was published by Thomas Nelson and Sons of the United Kingdom. The literary editor of the Nkrumah biography was Mrs. June Milne, the wife of Mr. John Milne, who represented the publishers in West Africa, with residence in the then Gold Coast. Mrs. Milne, the University of London-educated historian, continued to work for the late President Nkrumah as a literary editor and, in the end, he made her the literary executrix of all of his documents, some of which were later edited by her and published by Panaf Books Limited of London, a publishing company that Nkrumah instructed her to establish for that purpose.

Dr. Kyerematen was so busy setting up his National Cultural Centre in Kumasi, his native Ashanti regional capital, that he did not have the time to write either a memoir or an autobiography in which he could provide, for his readers, details about the fine educational institutions he was privileged to attend, also similar to what Dr. Nkrumah did in his 1957 autobiography, in which he discussed in detail Lincoln University, his undergraduate *alma mater* as well as University of Pennsylvania, his postgraduate *alma mater*, both in Pennsylvania, USA, and other institutions in the United Kingdom and his native Gold Coast.

To fulfill the wish of Dr. Kyerematen, as expressed by Mrs. Kyerematen-Darko, we have endeavored to provide information on each of the universities that her father attended, starting with Fourah Bay College in Sierra Leone, which has recently been facing some challenges. Apart from information from Dr. Kyerematen's records, including the diary that he scrupulously kept, we also relied on some public domain publications. These institutions played an important role in shaping his mind and ideas, which, in turn, were important in the preservation of cultural history in Ghana. Therefore, it is important to explore the institutional contexts which helped to shape his vision for Ghana, that is still unfolding today.

ADISADEL

Adisadel College, with Anglican Church affiliation, was established in 1910 in a building at Topp Yard, near Christ Church and the (in)famous Cape Coast Castle, which was used for commercial and slave trading. Although it currently has not less than 3,000 students, the college opened its doors with only 29 boys, but by 1935, it had about 200 male students. Although the name of the founder of the college was Templyn Hamlyn (the Anglican bishop resident in the Ghanaian capital of Accra), the school's physical infrastructure, including its buildings, were extended in 1950 by Maxwell Fry and Jane Drew. When it celebrated its golden jubilee in 1960, enrollment had gone up to 545. When the college observed its centenary in 2010, there were over 1,500 boys (all boarders), with 93 tutors.

As shown in the institution's records, Bishop Hamlyn established Adisadel College for the sole purpose of providing a grammar school-type education for sons of Anglican parents, in particular to serve as a training ground for church-related personnel and Christian missionaries. The institution that young Kyerematen attended is the second oldest secondary school in Ghana, and it is seen as one of the most famous institutions of learning in sub-Saharan Africa. The first secondary school to be established in the country—and also in Cape Coast area—was Mfantsipim School, which was founded by the Anglican church's competitor, the Methodist Church, in 1876.

Indeed, Adisadel College's customs and practices have amply demonstrated that tradition dies hard. For, it was the first secondary school in the history of the Gold Coast to have its prefects wear specially designed cloaks with red colors for the head prefect, blue for the other prefects and green for their assistants. The uniform of the school is a black and white shirt, with a pair of black shorts. It is commonly referred to as "zebra" for its resemblance to the skin of the zebra.

SPORTS AT ADISADEL

Sporting activities were intensified under Headmaster Alan Knight. Rugger i.e., Rugby football, was introduced and the interest that it generated almost eclipsed that of soccer. In cricket and athletics, the School reigned supreme in many competitions with other existing secondary schools, notably, Mfantsipim School, Achimota College and Accra Technical School. For the first time, the "Aggrey Shield," which had always been won by Achimota, was brought to Cape Coast by the St. Nicholas boys in 1934. Around this time, the School Ode, in which is enshrined the ideals, hopes and aspirations of the school, was composed and set to music by a student, Jack B. Wilmot. Does one doubt that the "Adisadel Spirit" was being born?

According to the former students, the early thirties were indeed the "moving" years of the now Adisadel College. The School's literary magazine, SANTACLAUSIANS made its debut and reflected the literary and creative excellence of the boys. Also, in appearance was a weekly newsletter, The OWL. This publication, managed and produced by a coterie of writers in the Upper forms, caused quite a stir with its forthright editorials, satirical comments, news tidbits, gossip, and poetry. The newsletter never spared those whom it believed were responsible for the lapses and shortcomings of the School. These publications continue to exist and serve the purposes of educating, informing and entertaining the boys. The OWL has grown to become an institution by itself and is usually exhibited in a glass case at a conspicuous position in front of the Assembly Hall.

There also existed, at one time, a publication known as "Fifth Form Review." This periodic publication had the effect of helping to develop the literary talents of the fifth formers, who aspired to journalistic or literary excellence. Then Father Knight, as the head of the institution, took a personal interest in his boys to the extent of "adopting" some of them. Those boys included J. K. Oppon and J.V.M. Ntow, whom he took along with him to England in his campaign to raise funds on behalf of Adisadel. (Victor Ntow, who later graduated B.A., and LL.B., taught at the college, thus later after leaving campus, and before furthering his education to become a barrister in the United Kingdom). If, indeed, the Topp Yard to Top Hill boys were "ever prepared" to help themselves, it was because of Father Knight, who was ably assisted by S. R. S. Nicholas, who provided the conducive atmosphere.

ACADEMIC IMPORTANCE AND GRADUATE TUTORS FOR DR. KYEREMATEN AND HIS CLASSMATES AT ADISADEL

The future Dr. A. A. Y. Kyerematen and his fellow Adisadel College students benefitted tremendously from high quality tutors and other instructors. For example, university graduates were recruited one after the other to teach in the School. At morning assemblies and in the classrooms, tutors were required to wear their graduation gowns. This fascinated most of the students, who consequently aspired to enter the university and obtain degrees after their formal education. It was an impressive spectacle to see the headmaster and some of his staff arrayed in their colourful academic robes especially on such occasions as Founder's Day and Visitation Day (otherwise known as the Speech and Prize-Giving Day) which are great social occasions on the calendar of the School.

The academic air that prevailed had its chain reactions. It produced a new crop of self-disciplined graduates. Some of the Old Boys who were then on the staff of the School set the ball rolling. They took every possible step to read for degrees of one sort or another through private tutorials and correspondence courses. There were no other facilities for university education available in the country. The future Dr. C. A. Ackah was the first to emerge with a B.A. (Hons) degree in Philosophy, followed by Albert Hammond, who notched a B.A. (Hons) in Classics, both as external candidates of the University of London.

True to the "Adisadel Spirit" of self-help, two Old Boys had achieved what was then considered almost impossible in the country. No doubt, these successes inspired other scholars, to emulate their examples. Those who followed their footsteps included A. M. L. Taylor and C. W. Sackeyfio. Having passed the Inter-B.A. examination locally as external students of the University of London, they both later went to Britain, the former to Oxford and the latter to Wales. They eventually returned home with B.A. (Hons) in Mathematics and B.A. (Hons) in Geography, respectively. Before them, another former tutor of the School, J. H. Amponsah, had similarly won his spurs, graduating B.A. (Hons) in Philosophy of the University of London.

DISTINCTIVE EDIFICES OF DR. KYEREMATEN'S COLLEGE (ADISADEL)

Our interviewees confirmed the adage that scholarship without religion is sterile. The strong religious foundation of the School has been duly emphasized at Adisadel and this is reflected in the imposing School Chapel erected on the side of the hill and overlooking the central compound. The Chapel, of a distinctive architectural design, is named after St. Nicholas, the Patron Saint of the School, and was built with donations and other contributions made by friends and well-wishers of the School, many of them in Britain. Another striking building is the Clock Tower, the gift of the Contractors who carried out the first phase of the project. Both edifices are built of reinforced concrete with impressive marble finishes.

In 1937, Father Knight went home with the aim of campaigning for more funds to further the college building programme. But he was destined not to return to his beloved Adisadel. For he was appointed Bishop of Georgetown in British Guiana (now Guyana) by the Archbishop of Canterbury, the Primate of all England, His Grace Cosmo Gordon Lang, D.D., obviously in recognition of his dedicated services and the "shining virtues of his head and heart." And so, a glorious and stirring chapter in the annals of Adisadel College was brought to a close.

FOURAH BAY COLLEGE, SIERRA LEONE

After attending the Cape Coast-based Adisadel College in the then Gold Coast (now Ghana since 1957), it was Fourah Bay College that the young Kyerematen attended initially for him to prepare for a British academic degree. It is a public university that is located in Mount Aureol area of Freetown, the capital of Sierra Leone, the West African country that the British created to resettle former slaves, similar to what freed slaves from America did in Liberia, a neighboring West African settlement for the freed slaves, who called themselves Americo-Liberians. Founded on 18th of February 1827, Fourah Bay College is considered the oldest university in West Africa and the first Western-style university built in Africa's sub-region south of the Sahara Desert. Currently, it is a constituent college of the University of Sierra Leone; formerly, it was affiliated with Durham University in the United Kingdom, from where the young Kyerematen earned his first degree in history. Professor Ibrahim Abdullah, a high school contemporary of Professor Ibrahim Gassama, who wrote the introduction to this book, wrote in a publicly distributed memorandum in June 2016 that the famous Fourah

Bay College, where he was serving as a professor, was reportedly facing a lot of difficulties due to various reasons, including a difference in leadership styles, and what he considered to be a want of leadership, which had been denied by his opponents.

In his public statement, Professor Abdullah felt that there was an urgent need for a thoughtful intervention in order to save Fourah Bay College from what he considers to be the institution's imminent "death." He cited various instances of contributing to the situation on the institution's campus. We are providing these brief pieces of information so that well-wishers may go to the aid of the great institution that served well for the formative years of the young Kyerematen from the Gold Coast.

Also, another well-meaning report, for example, underscored that failure for Fourah Bay College to move beyond its religious-*cum*-liberal arts under-graduate birthmark has meant that the college could not lay the foundation for the production and reproduction of a string of knowledge needed in an academic setting. Currently, the claim has been that every department of the institution was under-staffed and that professors as well as senior lecturers are few and far between. Also, it is being reported that the bulk of those who labored very hard at Fourah Bay College reportedly only have bachelor's and master's degrees but not the expected terminal academic qualifications (or degrees).

To Dr. Abdullah and others, the foregoing situation was unacceptable at the dawn of the twentieth century, which is described as the knowledge century. Before he passed away, the late Dr. Raymond Kamara, a pro-chancellor of the sister University of Sierra Leone, a national institution of higher learning, also raised his own alarm about the state of affairs at Fourah Bay College. He, in fact, appealed directly to the president of Sierra Leone to intervene, and we wonder what Dr. Kyerematen would have either said or done if he had been alive.

UNIVERSITY OF DURHAM

In his diary, Dr. Kyerematen lauded the coat of arms of University of Durham (or *Universitas Dunelmensis* in Latin). He also cherished the university's motto in Latin: "*Fundamenta eius super montibus sanctis*"; which reads in English as: "Her foundations are upon the holy hills." Dr. Kyerematen, in his student days' diary, referred to the institution as Durham University (but it is also known as the University of Durham). Furthermore, it is very often described as a college and a public research university, which is at Durham, in the North East part of England. It has a second campus in nearby town of Stockton-on-Tees.

As the available records and Dr. Kyerematen's notes have confirmed, the university was, in fact, put in place or established by an 1832 Act of the British Parliament, but it received its much-needed Royal Charter five years later, in 1837. It was one of the initial institutions of higher learning (or universities) to start offering classes in the United Kingdom over five hundred or more years ago as confirmed in University of Durham's historic records. Indeed, it happened to be the seventh-oldest university in the entire United Kingdom. Dr. Kyerematen was always proud of the university's estate, which includes 63 historic buildings; among the famous, as described in Dr. Kyerematen's recorded documents—including pocket diaries he kept—were the 11th-century Durham Castle as well as a 1930s' Art Deco chapel. The university, to the admiration of its graduates like the future Dr. Kyerematen, also did own as well the Durham World Heritage Site in partnership with the well-known Durham Cathedral. Former students like Dr. Kyerematen very much valued the historic and elaborate Cosin's Library of the university, which they used for their studies in order to excel.

The University of Durham has invariably ranked 6th among British universities. Therefore, Dr. Kyerematen—as its proud graduate—would have been very happy to read, if alive, that his undergraduate *alma* mater was Sports University of the Year for 2015, adjudged by *The Times of London* and *Sunday Times*, also of London.

KEBLE COLLEGE, OXFORD

Then enters in his biographical setting the famous and rich Keble College as, indeed, a constituent college of the famous University of Oxford, from where Dr. Kyerematen earned his first postgraduate degree. It is known in Latin as *Colleegium Keblense*, thanks to the college's well-kept records, some of which are noted in Dr. Kyerematen's documents. Known to have been founded in early 1870s, the institution was named after a British citizen by the name of John Keble; according to Oxford pairings, it also, it happens to be the sister college of Selwyn College of Cambridge University. Often with more undergraduate population that totaled not less than 400 students, its graduate (or postgraduate) students—which happened to include Dr. Kyerematen—are slightly more than 200 recruited or admitted students each academic year. Keble, has been constructed as a monument to Keble, who happened to be a very radical leading member of the Oxford Movement, known for its radical campus politics within the Oxford Union. Very interestingly, Keble's radical movement did either embody or stress the Roman Catholic aspect of the Church of England, too which the Royal Family usually belong and in which it worships. As expected, Keble College has very traditionally placed a considerable emphasis on theological teaching in the past. According to the available records, soon after World War II (WWII), the College placed a lot more emphasis on a curriculum that prided itself of scientific courses. At the time that Kyerematen attended Keble, he was one of a small number of Africans at the institution, which was, at the time, all male. In the 1970s, Keble introduced co-education for men and women and since that time, it has been doing more work in the area of racial inclusion. In April 2018, Keble College unveiled an oil portrait of Oxford Union's first African-Caribbean President, who was a contemporary of Alexander Kyerematen (https:// www.keble.ox.ac.uk/news/keble-unveils-portrait-oxford-unions-first-african -caribbean-president/).

KING'S COLLEGE, CAMBRIDGE

The famous King's College is a campus of the University of Cambridge, and it was from there that Dr. Kyerematen eventually earned his doctoral (D.Phil) degree in Anthropology. When the College was originally established, it was named as King's College of Our Lady and Saint Nicholas, and it was immediately made part of Cambridge University that, in Latinic terms like Oxford's Keble and pothers elsewhere, it is *known as Collegium Regale beate Marie et sancti Nicholai Cantebrigie*. Institutionally, it can be located near the Cam River. Geographically, it is not far from the center of the city of Cambridge, which has a history of its own, as having been established in 1441 by English King Henry VI; that happened soon after the King had also put in place the sister college known as Eton, which is a boys' college that many African male youngsters from wealthy families (including West Africa's late Nigeria-Biafra civil war hero by the name of Colonel Emeka Odumegwu Ojukwu) attended to prepare for prestigious British higher education; Ojukwu, for example, rightly prided himself as having attended University of Oxford, from here he studied History and, in the end, supposed to have earned a Master's degree in the subject. In fact, the building housing the college's famous chapel, which was started in 1446, was finally reported to have been completed in 1544, at the time that Henry VIII was on the English throne.

    Indeed, King's College, attended by Dr. Kyerematen, is regarded as one of the greatest examples of late Gothic English architecture. The college—supposed to have the world's largest fan-vault—has a chapel with stained-glass windows and wooden chancel screen. They are regarded as some of the finest from their era. The building is seen as emblematic of Cambridge. The chapel's choir, composed of male students is renowned in the world. Given Kyerematen's interest in culture and art, studying at King's College, which was rich in beautiful architecture and art, perhaps made him even more eager to study and return to Ghana where he could work with others to build similar institutions for his country.

As Dr. Kyerematen has noted in a diary that he kept religiously, each year during the memorable Christmas eve, there is the Festival of Nine Lessons and Carols, which is a service that is devised specifically for King's College by the College's Dean, and it is broadcast from the chapel to millions of listeners worldwide. King's College, indeed, offers all undergraduate courses available at the University, except for Education, Land Economy and Vet Medicine, although Directors of Studies for Anglo-Saxon Norse & Celtic and Management Studies visit from other colleges. With more than 100 fellows and some 420 undergraduate students, King's College has one of the highest ratios of fellows to students of all the Cambridge Colleges. Since its foundation, the college has housed a library, providing books for all students, covering all the subjects offered by King's. Around 130,000 books are held: some available for teaching and for reference, others being rare books and manuscripts. Special collections include a separate Music Library, the Keynes Library, a Global Warming collection, and an Audio Visual Library.

King's College of today—compared to when Dr. Kyerematen was there pursuing his doctorate in the field of Anthropology—has enlarged its intake to include many students from public schools of the United Kingdom and several British Commonweal nations, which are known to have included such African countries as the then Gold Coast (now Ghana), Sierra Leone, Nigeria and The Gambia. As noted in its records, the college very often had the highest level or proportion of its school acceptances in its undergraduate colleges.

During our research, a very interesting and also impressive scenario that we encountered was to learn that Dr. Kyerematen nursed the hope, for years as a student in the United Kingdom, to return to then Gold Coast at the time to make sure that his country's cultural heritage was preserved. In his three diaries, he recorded the interest. As the late daughter (Mrs. Bridget Kyerematen-Darko) explained to us, she was sure that her late father did record the interest that way and also talked about it to make sure that, if he did not live to implement it himself, someone else would, indeed, have carried it out. It has also been confirmed by individuals, who knew Dr. Kyerematen well –including Roman Catholic Archbishop Emeritus Sarpong—that they believed that he studied Cultural Anthropology in order to understand his people's culture, which was part of what the Ghana National Cultural Center was all about. In fact, very early on in Oxford, his thesis at Keble College was very much an anthropological nuance of his Ashanti people. Then, later on at Cambridge, he studied another aspect of the Ashanti culture for his doctoral (D. Phil) Dissertation.

Chapter 3

The Genesis of the Ghana National Cultural Centre

As Dr. Kyerematen Pictured a Noble Idea and Aim

A wise person once said that without vision, people perish. Our research on Dr. Kyerematen showed that he was definitely a man with noble aim and vision. Many individuals, who were familiar with the young Kyerematen, felt that he had a mental picture of the cultural edifice that he wanted to establish as a result of his newly acquired expertise and appreciation for culture in general. Therefore, as Daniel Appiah-Adjei of Kumasi wrote (and it is quoted in full in the appendices area of this book), by the time in the early 1950s that he (as the young Kyerematen) returned to the Gold Coast from his initial foreign junkets as a graduate of University of Durham in the United Kingdom, he had conceived in his mind a comprehensive program of activities that were aimed at putting life into the mental picture that he had of a cultural centre.

Although he did not immediately know its magnitude, he still needed to get it off the ground. That was why Appiah-Adjei aptly went on to quote Ama Ata Aidoo, the late celebrated and veteran female Ghanaian writer, from her memorable play, *The Dilemma of a Ghost*. He quoted: "The day of planning is different from the day of battle." Professor Aidoo was well-known for her other well-written play, *Anowa*. Subsequently, the young Kyerematen, as expected, discovered, to his utmost dismay, that it is one thing having a beautiful mental picture of what one wants to achieve, but it is another thing getting other people to offer the needed support in sharing one's vision.

In fact, most of the friends and acquaintances the young Kyerematen approached in Kumasi and other places to share his vision for the cultural centre sounded very friendly and outwardly sympathetic. However, nothing materialized beyond that. Some of them promised him everything but money;

however, he needed funds to lay the first foundation on which his mental picture would become a reality. The lukewarm attitude of his friends and admirers made things really gloomy.

THE GENESIS OF THE GHANA NATIONAL CULTURAL CENTRE: THE ASANTEMAN COUNCIL OF CHIEFS OF THE GOLD COAST GIVE A HELPING HAND

It started as the Asante Cultural Centre in 1952. At the time, Dr. Kyerematen was serving as the secretary of the Asante Confederacy Council, which was renamed that year as the Asanteman Council. Young Kyerematen made several attempts to secure the needed monetary help for the cultural centre that he had in mind, but all his plans and contacts proved fruitless. He therefore took a bold step and approached the Asanteman Council of Chiefs to convince the *Nananom* of the unlimited benefits that they and subjects of the Ashanti Kingdom would later derive from the proposed cultural centre. He simply sought an appointment for an audience with the eminent chiefs. As expected, Dr. Kyerematen's first attempt to speak with the chiefs about his plans to establish the cultural centre yielded desired expectations. The chiefs saw the hard work by the selfless young Kyerematen, so these august members of the Asanteman Council showed appreciation through monetary donations.

What they did was very creative, for they all decided to forego their sitting allowances—money received for attending the meeting—following their meeting with young Kyerematen that day as their donation to the project. This offer convinced Dr. Kyerematen of the interest these chiefs had in the cultural centre, a demonstration of the unity of the old Asante Kotoko spirit. It was the spirit of oneness that showed in times of difficulty and national crisis, harking back to when the Asantehene needed that sort of unity to raise armies for war.

With the initial donation from the council of chiefs, young Kyerematen knew that his battle was half won. He recognized that as time went on, he would be able to persuade the chiefs to give more. He did feel tired and weary, but was very happy that the Asanteman Council had bought into his plan to establish the cultural centre, a situation that gave him sound sleep that night. To show his seriousness about the project, young Kyerematen started in earnest to put in place active plans, contacting architects and building designers to involve them with the relevant activities in connection with the progress towards establishing the cultural centre. Indeed, not only was brilliance needed, for he had that, but sound judgement in the art of negotiation. It was here that young Kyerematen's humility, as an individual, came to light when he accepted an appointment to serve the Asanteman Council as its secretary. To avoid a conflict of interest, he declined the chairmanship of the Cultural

Centre Committee set up by the Asanteman Council to plan and execute the project, requesting that the position be assigned to someone else. However, Kyerematen took responsibility for organizing and publicizing meetings of the planning committee and keeping impeccable records of the project, coupled with handling the high volume of paperwork that he executed with great seriousness and efficiency.

The chiefs saw the outstanding manner with which young Kyerematen broadly displayed his impressive national and international outlook towards his people's culture. He made the chiefs know that to him, culture was a universal art from which everyone should derive some benefits through the cultural centre that he had in mind, regardless of race, creed, ethnicity, clan or political affiliation. That, indeed, was the true thinking of young Kyerematen.

OTUMFUO SIR OSEI AGYEMANG PREMPEH II: CATALYST FOR PROJECT IMPLEMENTATION

Records kept by the Asanteman Council have demonstrated amply that but for the unlimited support, the enthusiasm, and the blessings registered by the Asantehene of the day (Otumfuo Sir Osei Agyeman Prempeh II), young Kyerematen's entire project and his vision for a brand new cultural centre would have died a premature death. In his official capacities as the Asantehene and president of the Asanteman Council, the Otumfuo led the way for the project to start in earnest. His action stemmed from his unparalleled devotion to and interest in the establishment and viability of such a cultural centre.

It is also on record, thanks to Mr. Appiah-Adjei, the writer, that Otumfuo's keen interest in the establishment of the cultural centre surprised no one. After all, it was widely known that the Otumfuo—who occupied the powerful Golden Stool from June 22, 1931, to May 27, 1970—was, without any shade of doubt, the leading authority on the history and culture of his own Asante Kingdom; being very enlightened in his own way, he was credited with reviving Ashanti culture and bringing about the restoration of the unity of the Asante people, which had always been enshrined in the Golden Stool that he occupied.

To Nana Sir Otumfuo Osei Agyeman Prempeh II, the idea for the establishment of the cultural centre, which was named for the Ashanti Region of the country, was a welcome opportunity for him to strengthen the unity of the Asante people and, in the process, to demonstrate the legacy of some of the rich cultural heritage which their ancestors had left them. Toward the foregoing ends, the Asantehene made sure on July 5, 1951, to appoint a committee of six eminent Asante citizens and charged it with the following lofty terms of reference: to make recommendations to the Asanteman Council on the steps to be taken to establish the cultural centre, with the aims and objectives to include the preservation of Asante culture, the fostering of social research and publication of a journal containing notes on Asante customs and other matters of general interest. The efforts were commended in high and low places because they were deemed a wise decision, which was for not only the Ashantis but the entire Ghanaian nation. The country has continued to show great gratitude to the late Otumfuo and his councilors for their foresight.

The genesis of the center, which was to house the new museum, was captured in *Ghana National Cultural Center: A Twenty-One Year Old Cultural Experiment*, a 32-page publication published by University Press of Kumasi. The essential words, *inter alia*, were the following (Introduction): He [Dr. Kyerematen] realized that there was an urgent need for the preservation of [Ghana's] rich cultural heritage not only in writing but [also] in such concrete forms as museums, zoos, archives, theaters, craft centre for indigenous Ghanaian craftsmen, traditional music and dancing groups, drama groups and even a library, where books about [Ghanaian] arts and culture could be made readily available for any aspiring Ghanaian, who wanted to learn more about or research more into them. By the time Dr. Kyerematen returned to the former Gold Coast in 1950, he had drawn up a comprehensive program of activities aimed at putting life into this mental picture and getting its feet off the ground. The result is now the Ghana National Cultural Centre.

For five years, the plans for the cultural center progressed unabated. However, October 27, 1956, became a day to be remembered for a significant achievement, as it was on that day that people from all walks of life and all races gathered to witness the opening ceremony of the first phase of the Prempeh II Jubilee Museum by the Asantehene himself, Otumfuo Osei Agyeman Prempeh II. Many wondered that if the Asantehene had not tasked members of the project committee to work diligently, the throng of people at the October 1956 event, might not have dreamed of celebrating this important milestone. The museum was the first to be put up by the Building Committee on the site. Most certainly, what happened was a great triumph for the vision of young Kyerematen, as it was heavily supported by the Asantehene. The whole impetus ignited the passion of the young Kyerematen to act to promote the Asante culture, as he realized that there was an urgent need for the preservation of the rich cultural heritage of the Ashanti people and, later, the entire nation. As has been earlier stated, aside from the museum, there was to be a zoo, archives, theatres, craft centres for indigenous Ghanaian craftsmen and women (for which he acquired a large parcel of land at Wamase, which is a suburb of Kumasi, the home of the Ashanti cultural centre); it was to include traditional music and dance groups, drama groups and a library or bookstore, where books about Ashanti arts and culture could be made readily available for aspiring Ghanaians, who wanted to learn more about or research more into their own cultural heritage, thanks to the young Kyerematen.

INITIAL NAME: ASANTE CULTURAL CENTRE

Young Kyerematen consulted with the Asantehene (Otumfuo Sir Osei Agyeman Prempeh II) and his Asanteman Council about a proper name for the mutual project. It was unanimously agreed that it was to be named Asante Cultural Centre. This was its name until 1963, when the first elected Ghanaian president, Osagyefo Dr. Kwame Nkrumah, on an official visit to Tamale, stopped at the Asante Cultural Centre. He was impressed with the fact that he shared with young Kyerematen a vision of a national cultural centre, so decided to support the new centre financially. President Nkrumah and centre Director Kyerematen, in consultation with the Otumfuo, agreed on a new name for the venue, Ghana National Cultural Centre. As has been previously explained, this name sufficed until the National Redemption/Supreme Military Council (NRC/SMC) ordered a name change. Later in 1990, the Provisional National Defense Council (PNDC) revised Ghana's cultural policy, which led to the decentralization of the cultural centre, the effect of which saw the cultural centre again being renamed Centre for National Culture, Kumasi branch. The change in designation meant that similar centres would be established at all regional capitals.

ASANTEHENE'S PROMOTION OF
THE CULTURAL CENTRE

Since Otumfuo Nana Sir Osei Agyeman Prempeh II tried to eschew partisan politics of any kind, he did not get involved in the name changes for the cultural centre. Instead, he always assured the young Kyerematen of his staunch support. A practical demonstration of his support came in 1970, when for the first time in the history of the Asantehene's Manhyia Palace, the Otumfuo decided to observe, in a big way, his *Akwasidae* Festival at the National Cultural Centre. Had the festival taken place, the reigning Asantehene would have exhibited a better proof of his devotion for and a keen interest in the centre. However, it was widely speculated that the Asantehene was unwell at the time, and the plans for the festival at the centre were called off. Sadly, on May 27, 1970, Otumfuo joined his ancestors, as he passed away before the festival could be held. Following the passing of the Asantehene, the centre still maintains its original name as the Ghana National Cultural Centre, but it was deemed appropriate to rename the museum the Nana Prempeh II Museum.

A WORD ABOUT OTHER CENTRE SUPPORTERS

There is the prayer that one day, the cultural centre will be named for either Dr. Kyerematen or the late Asantehene, Nana Sir Otumfuo Osei Agyeman Prempeh II, who as has just been recounted, played a yeoman's role in its establishment. When he is so honored with the renaming of the centre, then it will fulfil former centre Director Nana Brefo Boateng's appeal in a public speech for such honors to be rendered. In terms of personalities, who played major roles for the birth of the venture, including its teething years and growth, many names pop up in the records. Dr. Kyerematen must receive great gratitude for listing the names of individuals, groups, organizations and companies, without whose assistance the history of the Kumasi-based cultural centre would not have been completed. Among these active promoters were the following: Honorable Mr. Justice S. O. Quarshie-Idun, a Senior High Court Judge in Kumasi, who was appointed as an early chairman of the Building Committee of the proposed Asante Cultural Centre after the death of the first chairman, the late Nana Akwasi Afrane III, Ejisuhene; Nana Yaw Sarpong II, Juabenhene; Mr. J. H. Gambrah; Mr. D. J. Buahen; Mr. N. Abubakar; Mr. B. E. Dwira; Mr. C. F Amoo; Bafour Osei Akoto, the Asantehene's Senior Linguist; Professor A. W. Lawrence (KNUST); Mrs. Mary Asimaku-Idun; Mr. J. S. Miller; Mr. W. A. Boateng; the distinguished author and wife of Lawyer Joe Appiah, Mrs. Peggy Appiah; Dr. Ephraim Amu (the distinguished musician); Professor A. Mawere Opoku (Dance Choreographer); Mr. A. Y. Berkoe; Mr. J. O. Pumpuni; J. C. Roberts; J. K. Frimpong; Mr. Kojo Affrani; Mr. Kwasi Berchie; J. Collingwoods William; M. A Mekano; Mr. S. K. Danso (city councillor), Mr. A. G. Ampadu; Mr. Moses Boamah; Mr. G. K. Appiah; Mr. A. K Amissah; Mr. J. K. Antwi; Mr. R. N. Barfour-Awuah; Mr. Edward Donkor; Mr. James Owusu (City Council Chairman); Madam Ama Kwaadu (direct descendant of Okomfo Anokye of the famous Golden Stool); Dr. R. P. Barfour (who donated money for the erection of the crafts shop on behalf of the University of Science and Technology, now known as the Kwame Nkrumah University of Science and Technology [KNUST]); Mrs. J. O. Marles; Mrs. Rhoda Mead; Mr. A. Duku; Mr. J. H. K. Folson; Mr. R. O. Amoako-Atta (regional commissioner under the Nkrumah regime); Nana Atakora Amaniampong II, the then Mamponghene; Dr. Dsane Selby; Mr. Owusu Ansah, former Regional Minster of Ashanti; A. E. Nkansa-Dwamena; Dr. Seth Cudjoe; Nana Kwantwi Barima II, Adansehene; Prof. E. V. Asihene; L. K. Idan; Kingsley Obeng; K. Danso-Manu; R. A. Frimpong; and Ms. Adelaide Amagatcher.

CENTRE'S FINANCIAL/MATERIAL DONORS

Apart from the Asanteman Council, headed by the Asantehene, several companies and organizations also made monetary and material donations for the welfare and growth of the cultural centre that Dr. Kyerematen founded and ably led. From his impeccable records, among the firms/organizations and individuals who made such contributions and rendered other services to the centre are the following: Messrs. A. Lang and Company (£2,000) towards the construction of the Kumasi Zoo; the Lebanese Community of Kumasi, headed by Mr. A. Daniel, for building the Dwaberem or Open-Air Theatre of the center; the Swiss African Trading Company, headed by Mr. Hans Roth, for constructing the Independence Exhibition Hall of the center; Messrs J. Monta and Sons and the University of Science and Technology for providing services on architecture and engineering consultancy; Messrs A. D. C Hyland; W. Timpo; Dr. F. O. Kwami (Engineer); Dr. N. D. Sodzi; Messrs. S. O. Larbi; Richard Stappleton; F. K. Akwaboa; C. W. Claur; C. Mahadevan; A. G. Ameyaw; S. Yanney; S. L. Quartey; S. Y Danso; and John Logosu. Furthermore, Mr. Owen Barton of the regional Ministry of Education and Social Welfare and the others named donated to the establishment of the center, sometimes directly through Dr. Alexander Atta Yaw Kyerematen, the director. Benefactors who passed away soon after making donations to the center included Opanin Kwasi Penkwa; Opanin Kwabena Asare; Opanin Kobina Eduonu; Mr. Christopher Holm; Nana Obiri Yeboah; Mr. Yeboa Nyamekye; Mr. S. Abdulai Alhassan; Mr. M. M. Arthur; Bob Okyeadee; Mr. Attakora Gyimah (journalist at *Pioneer* newspaper, Kumasi); and Wofa Attah. May they have eternal and peaceful rest in the Lord.

It is also on record that Dr. Kyerematen left Ghana for the United Kingdom in 1965 to complete his doctoral dissertation at King's College of the University of Cambridge. Although the Asanteman Council assisted him in 1946 to attend Durham University—also in the United Kingdom—to complete his degree in history, this time around, he received a merit scholarship in the form of a postdoctoral fellowship from the International African Institute (IAI). The stipulation was that, upon the completion of the thesis, which was titled "Ashanti Royal Regalia: An Ethno-History of Ashanti Kingship"—the IAI would have the first option of publishing the doctoral work (or manuscript) as a book for assisting him with the scholarship. It was after receiving his doctorate that this illustrious son of Ghana was referred to as Dr. Alexander Atta Yaw Kyerematen.

Dr. Kyerematen Forges A Viable Working Relationship With The Ashanti King (Asantehene)

When Dr. Kyerematen needed a sizeable parcel of land to establish the then Kumasi Cultural Center, the King of Ashanti (Otumfuo Sir Nana Osei Tutu Agyeman Prempeh II) came to his rescue. Interestingly, he gave him prime land in the Bantama-Kejetia section of Kumasi. That, indeed, was not only a gracious act on the part of the King in terms of donating parcels of land for public good. For example, in 1948–1949, the King donated a large parcel of land for the establishment of a prestigious boys Secondary School (similar to an American High School), which came into existence in 1949 and was named Prempeh Secondary School (sometimes referred to as Prempeh College, with green and gold as its colors). The *Asantehene* would subsequently donate a new parcel of land for the establishment of a modern university, as part of Sir Agyeman Prempeh II's plans at modernizing his Ashanti Kingdom.

It was, in fact, in 1949, that the dream of the Ashanti King was realized when the buildings for what was initially known as Kumasi Cultural Center became a reality when the campus was built on land provided by the King for what initially became the Kumasi College of Technology. It offered admission to its first freshman class of students in an engineering degree program in 1951, with plans for classes to begin on January 22, 1952, as it needed an Act of Parliament to provide the statutory approval for what became as the Kumasi College of Technology; its new students included a teacher training college. For a start, the new college became a constituent degree-granting college of University of London for several years until 1961, when the college was granted its full status as a *bona fide* university. The land given for the construction of the college by the King of Ashanti is not less than 25,00 acres. Currently, it has been renamed Kwame Nkrumah University of Science and Technology (KNUST) in honor of the late President Kwame Nkrumah of Ghana. Among its famous graduates is former United Nations Secretary-General Kofi Annan (1938–2018) as well Mrs. Bridget Kyerematen-Darko, the daughter of Dr. Kyerematen. Her father served the Kwame Nkrumah University of Science and Technology (KNUST) in a variety of roles, including being elected as the Chairman of the University Council.

It was not very surprising that Sir Agyeman Prempeh II, the King of Ashanti, was honored with an honorary Doctor of Science degree in 1969, a year before he died. Currently, one of his successors, Otumfuo Nana Osei Tutu II, the Ashanti King, serves as the titular Chancellor of the Kwame Nkrumah University of Science and Technology (KNUST). Therefore, it was very much appreciated by the university's leaders that Ghana's President Nana Addo Dankwa Akufo-Addo and the Asantehene, Otumfuo Osei Tutu

II, deemed it auspicious to send prompt messages to congratulate Professor (Mrs.) Rita Akosua Dickson on her elevation and also investiture as the 11th Vice-Chancellor of the Kwame Nkrumah University of Science and Technology (KNUST), and the first woman to hold the position.

EARLY CENTRE DIRECTORS

Among those interviewed for this book are some of the former and current directors of the center, who were immediately available. It is a fact that, through their hard work, the centre has marked a lot of successes. In fact, some of them began with Dr. A. A. Y. Kyerematen, but they still served for a longer period after he passed away. They include Mr. W. Otchere-Darko, an assistant secretary during the first National Festival for Arts and Culture, which was facilitated and chaired by Dr. Kyerematen himself. Among past directors to be remembered are: Dr. Osei Kofi; Nana Brefo Boateng; Mr. Kwaku Owusu Akyiaw (who was interviewed for this publication); and the present director, Mr. S. F. Adjei (who was also interviewed for this publica- tion). They are gratefully acknowledged. Mr. Appiah-Adjei, the insightful writer on the centre, in thanking most of these individuals, aptly cites Étienne De Grellet, who once said: "I expect to pass through this world but once; any good thing therefore that I can do, or any kindness that I can show to any fel- low creature, let me do it now; let me not defer or neglect it; for I shall not pass this way again."

Dr. Kyerematen's close attachment to the Asantehene, Otumfuo Sir Osei Agyeman Prempeh II, facilitated his access to the land he needed to build the cultural edifice of his dream. On July 5th of that year, the Asanteman Council—which had the Asantehene, Nana Prempeh, as its president— appointed a six-person committee with a term of reference which read: "To make recommendations to the Council on the steps to be taken to establish a Centre, whose aims and objectives would include the preservation of Ashanti culture, the fostering of social research and publication of a journal contain- ing notes on Ashanti customs and other matters of general interest."

While the committee's work was going on, the Asantehene, Nana Prempeh, showed his full support for Dr. Kyerematen's request for the land. "Not only did His Majesty provide him [Dr. Kyerematen] with land, but also assisted financially to enable him to start this laudable dream of his," (Editor, 1986). It was on November 6th, of the same year, that the committee's report was published recommending to the Asanteman Council that the functions of the new centre should "include the services of a community centre and also made recommendations on the number and approximate cost of buildings required, sources of funds and organization of the center when established. It stressed the advisability of making the project the responsibility of the community as a whole and avoiding the tendency which would make the Centre appear as if it stood only for the people of Ashanti birth. It finally suggested the setting up of a larger Committee to be responsible for the raising of funds and all matters connected with the erection of the Centre's buildings."

To fulfill the recommendations of this committee, the Asantehene prompted Mr. J. A. Opoku, O.B.E., and the head of the Asantehene's Land Department, to offer a suitable site for the project. In fact, Mr. Opoku personally chaired the inaugural public meeting at Prempeh Assembly Hall to launch the fundraising for the project. A suitable message was sent from the Asantehene, which read in part: "It is with real pleasure that I send my good wishes for the success of the campaign through which funds are to be raised for the Asante Cultural Centre. I am aware of the many appeals made to the public for the support of such voluntary services, but I have no doubt that all to whom this appeal is made will respond generously, in view of the very important role that the Centre is to play in the social life of our community. Much is being done for the political and economic advancement of the country and cultural and spiritual development should not be neglected. It is in this latter objective that the Centre and similar institutions can serve so great a purpose. To the members of the Building Committee, the organizers of this campaign and all, who have already donated to the Building Fund, I say well done and may your efforts be an inspiration to others."

The Asantehene, Nana Prempeh, added that the project provided a unique opportunity for demonstrating the doctrine of self-help to show that it was so vital for a young country like ours with many developmental schemes to attend to." To demonstrate his full support for the cultural center project, Otumfuo Sir Osei Agyeman Prempeh II decided in 1970 to celebrate his *Akwasidae* Festival, for the first time, at the Centre. Sadly, his ill-health worsened, so the celebration was called off. He died soon after that. Before his death, the Asantehene had appointed Ejisuhene, Nana Kwasi Afrani III to head the Building Committee of the Asante Cultural Centre, but when he died, he was succeeded by an illustrious jurist, the Honorable Mr. Justice S. O. Quarshie-Idun (who was born on January 15, 1902, at Cape Coast, the region from where Dr. Kyerematen attended Adisadel College). There were several other committee members.

Nana Yaw Sarpong II, Juabenhene, was appointed chairman of the committee of six set up by the Asanteman Council to recommend further ways and means of keeping up with the plans to establish the remaining portion of the cultural center. Other committee members were Mr. J. H. Gambrah, who later headed the Appeals Fund Sub-Committee; Mr. D. J. Buahin; Mr. N. Abubakar; M. B. E. Dwira, Chairman of the Kumasi Municipal Council; and Dr. A. A. Y. Kyerematen, as honorary secretary.

While pondering over his next steps, Dr. Kyerematen accepted in the later part of 1952, a fellowship from the United Nations' Institute for Training and Research (UNITAR), which took him to the United States of America and Canada on what was categorized as a study tour. Through the fellowship, he was able to interest people and organizations in both countries in the cultural project he was starting back in the Gold Coast. What began as the Asante Cultural Centre was started in modesty but there was a serious approach towards its success by its founder, Dr. Kyerematen.

To give it a national stature, Dr. Kyerematen had a meeting with Ghana's President Nkrumah in 1962, during which the Ghanaian leader requested that the Asante Cultural Centre should be renamed as a National Cultural Centre, with the Convention People's Party government of the president providing the centre with regular financial support.

CULTURAL CENTRE'S DEPARTMENTS

It was deemed necessary, for administrative and other practical reasons, to devise the centre and its structures into various segments, including a museum, which was officially opened in 1956 by the late Asantehene (Nana Prempeh). As a living testimony to his devotion, interest and progress for the centre, the new museum was named the Sir Osei Agyeman Prempeh II Museum. Before the museum was constructed, the National Cultural Centre Library was established in July of 1954 by the Gold Coast Library Board. It had lending, reference, children's sections, a reading room and offices for the employees. The records have demonstrated that the projects for the centre were to be completed in phases, with the edifices already completed becoming part of phase one. The remaining phases were to include a rear exhibition and side and front galleries, in addition to a front balcony extension. All the foregoing structures were meant to represent all the ethnic groups of Ghana.

The support that Dr. Kyerematen sought, during his overseas trips, yielded results. For example, the Ford Foundation based in New York contributed 6,000 Ghana cedis towards the construction of projects within the second phase of the centre. The leaders of the funding committee expressed gratitude to the foundation for its gift. In fact, the funds enabled the centre to open the following segments.

DWABEREMKESEE (MEETING PLACE)

This edifice has been described as a well-kept lawn equipped with a raised dais for a traditional leader to sit and receive homage from his subjects. It was there that the former head of state of Ghana, General I. K. Acheampong, executed in 1979, was honored by the National House of Chiefs at a durbar held during the National Festival of Arts.

The Kumasi Zoo

In fact, the Kumasi Zoo was part of the project to be completed by the centre's committee. The Asantehene provided not less than 28 acres of land for the zoo project alone, while the design for it was completed by the superintendent of the London Zoo, George Cansdale. The Kumasi Zoo, which attracted visitors in its heyday from far and nearby places, is made up of (i) shallow pits with surrounding walls for reptiles, including crocodiles, snakes, pythons, and tortoises; (ii) a house-shaped theater, with an open-air enclosure. President Nkrumah declared the zoo officially opened for business on October 11, 1958, a year after Ghana's independence.

Exhibition Hall & Fountain

This establishment was made up of the Independence Exhibition Hall and an ornamental drinking fountain. They cost 7,000 Ghana cedis and 2,800 Ghana cedis, respectively. They were among the monuments erected to observe Ghana's independence anniversary of March 6, 1957. Also included as part of the Cultural Centre were the following: Ghana Goods Hall; Theater and Dance Arena (*Dwaberemkumaa*); Crafts Shop; a Reconstructed Village (Anokye Komanmu or Shrine); Amamereson Ahenfie, symbolizing a typical Ashanti chief's palace; the Patakesee; the Open-Air Chapel; Oratory (*Adikanfo Akrafieso*); and Quarshie-Idun Hall. A Crafts Village, which was intended to encourage the indigenous crafts of Ghana, was added later.

THE INITIAL IMPACT OF THE THEN NATIONAL CULTURAL CENTRE OF GHANA

In a span of ten years, from 1952 to 1962, Dr. Kyerematen had in place the initial Asante Cultural Centre, which he founded as a modest effort to be expanded later. During the period, the Asantehene (or King of the Asante or Ashanti people), the late Otumfuo Sir Osei Agyeman Prempeh II and his Asanteman Council of very able Ashanti chieftains, supported Dr. Kyerematen materially and morally. It was interesting that the first chairman of the Ghana National Commission on Culture of the ruling Provisional National Defence Council (PNDC), arbitrarily "decided to change the name from Ghana National Cultural Centre to Centre for National Culture [ostensibly] to correspond with other centers throughout the regions in Ghana," (p. 13). Yet, the impact of the center was felt throughout the Ashanti Region and beyond, and the reason was explained in *30 Years into Eternity* in the following words:

Dr. Kyerematen's view on culture was rather broad, contending that the cultural center in Kumasi did not only contain replicas of the regalia of traditional rulers but, also, the specimens of the main elements of the material culture of Ghana. (p. 13)

THE OXFORD, ADISADEL AND CAPE COAST CONNECTIONS: ADVOCATES FOR GHANA'S CULTURAL CENTER

Not only did the Oxford education help to enlighten Dr. Kyerematen, but it also provided him with connections to powerful allies, who would serve as advocates for the center. They included Alex Quaison-Sackey, then Archbishop Peter Akwasi Sarpong and the late prime minister K.A. Busia. Each of them played unique roles in the advocacy of the Centre as outlined below. Additionally, several other African political and scholarly giants have used the centre in ways that advanced its goals or as resources for their own political gains. The section below outlines the various connections to Dr. A.A.Y. Kyerematen and how they impacted the centre and its politics.

DR. ALEX QUAISON-SACKEY

Among a selected number of former college acquaintances to be interviewed for this publication was Dr. Alex Quaison-Sackey; he very happily, agreed to be interviewed about Dr. Kyerematen and the center he worked very hard to establish and to direct very efficiently for several years until Ghana's late President Kwame Nkrumah became aware of and decided to assist the center.

Dr. Quaison-Sackey, who was a close friend of the late President Nkrumah, was very familiar with the cultural interests of the then Ghanaian leader, dating back to 1962, the year that Nkrumah met center Director Kyerematen in Kumasi. Although Dr. Quaison-Sackey was serving as Ghana's Ambassador to the United Nations, with concurrent postings to Mexico and Cuba, President Nkrumah mentioned to him about the importance of the cultural centre in Kumasi, which he insisted on convincing its founder to convert to make it become the Ghana National Cultural Centre. On his part, Nkrumah also agreed to provide monetary subvention for its upkeep. Professor A. B. Assensoh had the pleasure of interviewing former Ambassador Quaison-Sackey during a visit to Accra, capital of Ghana; the initial interview was like killing two birds with one stone: to interview him about the late Black Muslim icon, Malcolm X, between 1990 and 1991, with the assistance of late Ambassador Kofi Awoonor. It was during this occasion that Assensoh was also able to get ex-Ambassador Quaison-Sackey to discuss at length about the life of Dr. Kyerematen, his fellow graduate of the University of Oxford.

Dr. Quaison-Sackey was born in 1933 at Winneba, in the Central Region of Ghana, and was 17 years younger than Dr. Kyerematen. However, they knew each other because of their Oxford backgrounds and later, also through discussions with Dr. Nkrumah. Their high school education was in Cape Coast, also in the Central Region. Although Dr. Kyerematen attended Adisadel College, Dr. Quaison-Sackey, however, received his early secondary education from Mfantsipim School, an institution that was variously similar to Adisadel College. It was from both of these institutions in Cape Coast, very much known for a cluster of very decent male and female secondary schools in the Central Region of Ghana, that they proceeded to study outside the then Gold Coast. While Dr. Kyerematen went to Fourah Bay College first in Sierra Leone, Dr. Quaison-Sackey studied for his honors first degree from Exeter College of University of Oxford. It was later on that he studied International Relations at the London School of Economics.

As a young man from the Gold Coast, Dr. Quaison-Sackey entered Exeter College, an affiliate of the University of Oxford—just like Ghana's former President John Agyekum Kufuor, who studied philosophy, politics and economics (the famous PPE). He subsequently began his diplomatic career, as one of Ghana's first Foreign Service officers in President Nkrumah's government. Ambassador Quaison-Sackey had an illustrious diplomatic career, thanks to a solid education. While Dr. Kyerematen worked privately on the cultural centre, between 1959 and 1965, Dr. Quaison-Sackey served at the United Nations as Ghana's Ambassador and Permanent Representative, a period which saw him elected as the first black president of the United Nations' General Assembly (1964–1965) as well as being concurrently accredited as Ambassador to Cuba. The Convention People's Party government of President Nkrumah—which had started to assist Dr. Kyerematen's cultural centre—was by 1966 facing several local and international challenges for ideological and Cold War reasons. Dr. Nkrumah, therefore, needed Dr. Quaison-Sackey back in Ghana for political support. Consequently, he (Dr. Quaison-Sackey) was named as Ghana's foreign minister in 1965, but the appointment was short-lived, as the new military leaders of Ghana, which had succeeded in toppling the Nkrumah regime on February 24, 1966, ended Dr. Quaison-Sackey's position, and he was replaced by someone else.

In fact, as a close ally and counsel to the deposed Ghanaian President (Dr. Nkrumah), Dr. Quaison-Sackey had travelled with the Ghanaian leader to China in February of 1966 when the Ghana coup d'état took place back in the capital, Accra. Interestingly, the former United Nations diplomat and, now in-charge of Ghana's foreign Affairs, was dispatched to the Ethiopian capital of Addis Ababa by Dr. Nkrumah, his boss, to challenge the credentials of Ghana's new military leaders at the 1966 annual meeting of the Organization of African Unity (OAU), the then continental organization that is now called the African Union (AU), still with its headquarters in Addis Ababa. Unfortunately for the deposed President Nkrumah, instead of Dr. Quaison-Sackey representing his deposed government as the *bona fide* Ghana representative, he wisely chose to return to Accra, the Ghanaian capital, and was reputed to have said on his return that he was breathing the air of true freedom due to the overthrow of the Nkrumah regime, which was seen by many Ghanaian citizens as being repressive (Nkrumah, 1968).

From the interview, it became known that the late President Nkrumah had discussed his prior interest in the cultural centre, but he waited for an opportunity to meet Dr. Kyerematen in person. According to Dr. Quaison-Sackey, the late Ghanaian President saw the centre as an embodiment of cultural awareness, which deserved governmental assistance. However, he did not want to be levelled as a dictator, who rushed to seize the private enterprise of Dr. Kyerematen. Then, the opportunity came, as Dr. Quaison-Sackey disclosed.

QUAISON-SACKEY, NKRUMAH AND THE CENTRE

Being very close to then President Nkrumah, Dr. Quaison-Sackey knew a lot about the support his boss gave to several Ghana-based private and semi-private organizations, including Dr. Kyerematen's cultural centre. It was therefore, taken seriously when he disclosed that the Ghanaian leader (President Nkrumah) was glad that Dr. Kyerematen did not politicize the cultural centre he had established in Kumasi, with the initial support from the reigning Asantehene at the time, Nana Sir Otumfuo Agyeman Prempeh II. For example, he was able to obtain prime land from the Asantehene (as explained in Chapter II) to establish the Ghana National Cultural Center, which was initially known as the Kumasi Cultural Center.

Sometimes, some observers and researchers on the cultural center wondered if the Asantehene (Sir Otumfuo) agreed to offer assistance because of Dr. Kyerematen's status. Yet, it was simply a sheer coincidence that he (Dr. Kyerematen) happened to hail from the royal house of Pataase, near Kumasi, where he eventually became the Chief (*Odikro*) before he died. Dr. Quaison-Sackey, who described President Nkrumah as a culturally sensitive and astute leader disclosed that Nkrumah was fascinated by the impressive work that Dr. Kyerematen was doing at his cultural center with limited resources available to him. That, indeed, was part of the Ghanaian leader's decision to assist the founder financially from the national coffers. It did, as a result, make sense that then President Nkrumah encouraged Dr. Kyerematen, as a founder of the centre, to rename it as the Ghana National Cultural Centre of Ghana, just as mentioned elsewhere in this book.

Dr. Quaison-Sackey intimated to Dr. A. B. Assensoh, during his interview with him, that when he visited Ghana in 1963 from the United Nations headquarters in New York, for consultations with Dr. Nkrumah, he indicated that it would be immensely beneficial to Ghana were Dr. Kyerematen to be appointed to head a cabinet-level position to administer cultural affairs. However, the former Ambassador opined that "Dr. Kyerematen won't touch that because he wanted to remain nonpolitical" (1963 Interview). Professor Assensoh asked Dr. Quaison-Sackey if Dr. Kyerematen was ever in danger of being associated with Ghana's future Prime Minister Kofi Abrefa Busia, a bitter political foe of the Ghanaian leader at the time. During that time, Dr. Busia was in self-imposed exile in Europe, in fact, later on at Oxford, from where he verbally attacked Nkrumah in interviews for destroying Ghana with his socialist policies. Coincidentally, the late Sociology Professor Busia—just like Dr. Kyerematen—was an Akan as well as an Oxford gradu-ate. Dr. Quaison-Sackey, who appeared intrigued by my question, laughed heartily and responded, *inter alia*: "In that case all of us would have been in trouble because I was an Oxford graduate, and so was Willie Abraham, who was a member of the Osagyefo's study group, indeed, his inner circle intellectually." According to Dr. Quaison-Sackey the differences between Dr. Nkrumah and Dr. Busia were deeper politically as well as ethnically. He explained that, in his opinion, it started in the 1940s when Nkrumah, as a young American-educated Gold Coast citizen, arrived in the United Kingdom and he at the time needed a prominent Gold Coast citizen to vouch, in writing, for his nationality and credentials to enable him enter the Inns of Court in London to begin his legal studies. The future Ghanaian leader felt that law would be useful for the future political interests that he harbored. "I think, he approached Kofi [Dr. Busia], and he declined to vouch for him, and reasonably so, as he did not know him from Adam," Dr. Quaison-Sackey pointed out.

Nkrumah would not reveal that fact publicly. Dr. Quaison-Sackey responded that both men, in spite of their political differences, were civil with each other, adding that those who needed to know were aware that the ani-mosity that seemed to exist between Ghana's two political giants—Nkrumah and Busia—was deeper than what was known publicly and politically. Professor Assensoh also wondered if Dr. Quaison-Sackey favored the renam-ing of the National Culture Centre in honor of Dr. Kyerematen.

In his opinion, it would have been wonderful if such a step was taken to immortalize the name of Dr. Kyerematen, whom he described as a visionary. However, Dr. Quaison-Sackey again stated that because of his familiarity with Dr. Kyerematen as a fellow Adisadel College "Old Student" (or graduate), he would assert that Dr. Kyerematen would have either been too modest or even uncomfortable to have the cultural centre named in his honor. The former ambassador said that because of the tangible assistance that he received from either the Asantehene, with respect to land, and the financial support of the Nkrumah government, maybe Dr. Kyerematen would have favored renaming the centre in honor of either the Ashanti king or the Ghanaian president. Plans were made for us, as co-authors, to visit Dr. Quaison-Sackey for a further interview about Dr. Kyerematen. Sadly, Ambassador Kofi Awoonor—who had helped the co-author strike up a personal relationship with Dr. Quaison-Sackey—informed him that the Ambassador had died at the Korle Bu Hospital in Accra, Ghana, in 1992 after suffering from blood clots (or described medically as pulmonary embolism).

EMERITUS ROMAN CATHOLIC ARCHBISHOP PETER AKWASI SARPONG

Another University of Oxford-educated Ghanaian the co-authors interviewed for this publication was archbishop emeritus of Kumasi, the Most Reverend Peter Akwasi Sarpong, who was born at Masse Offinso in the Ashanti Region of Ghana in 1933, 17 years after Dr. Kyerematen. The interview was at his retirement home near St. Hubert Minor Seminary in Kumasi, close to the Opoku Ware Secondary School; both institutions had Catholic religious influence.

Although Bishop Sarpong also attended Oxford, his preparation for entering this prestigious British institution was different from that of Dr. Kyerematen. Rather than attending a regular secondary school, the retired Archbishop studied at St. Peter's Regional Seminary at Cape Coast—again, also in the Central Region like Adisadel College—before being ordained as a Catholic priest in 1959 and subsequently attending the University of St. Thomas Aquinas in Rome. After young Rev. Sarong did postgraduate studies in Anthropology to earn a master's degree, he enrolled at the University of Oxford and for his doctoral degree, this time, in the area of Social Anthropology. Dr. Assensoh recalls that when doing his interview with the retired Catholic prelate about Dr. Kyerematen, he informed the Archbishop that he was also at Oxford on a postdoctoral fellowship, during which he (Assensoh) led two seminars at St. John's College. This piqued the bishop's interest, as he sought to know about some of the scholars the professor had interacted with. When Dr. Assensoh told Archbishop Sarpong that he gave his two seminars under the tutorship of the late Professor Edwin Ardener, the Archbishop confirmed that Ardener directed his dissertation at the University of Oxford. It was upon his return to Ghana from Oxford that Dr. Sarpong became the first African to hold the post of rector at St. Peter's Regional Seminary, Cape Coast. Then, in 1969, he became bishop of Kumasi. In 2002 Bishop Sarpong was consecrated as the metropolitan archbishop of Kumasi, and he retired in 2008.

Armed with a doctoral degree in anthropology, just like Dr. Kyerematen, the Archbishop Emeritus is known to have embarked on a variety of projects to help with Ghana's socio-economic, educational, religious and health sectors. They included the renovation of several Catholic-affiliated schools and the establishment of the St. Hubert Minor Seminary in Kumasi, not far from the pre-eminent Catholic-affiliated Opoku Ware Secondary School. While Dr. Kyerematen invested his expertise and energy in cultural matters, the Archbishop Emeritus is credited with the establishment of seven rural health clinics and has encouraged the development of cooperative credit unions throughout his diocese. Just like Dr. Kyerematen, the retired Archbishop has travelled widely, lecturing on different subjects during his travels. He has authored several very meaningful publications, some of which are similar thematically to those by Dr. Kyerematen. For example, some of the Archbishop's publications delve into culture and indigenous puberty rites. In our interview with him, the Catholic prelate remembered, with disappointment, efforts by some fellow Ghanaians to undermine the useful work of Dr. Kyerematen as a Ghanaian cultural guru.

An example, cited by the Emeritus Archbishop, was the fact that the head of culture of the ruling military regime, at the time, paid a brief courtesy visit to the vast cultural center that Dr. Kyerematen had labored to build and head. Presumably, the government official expected to see some particular cultural artifacts at the center but, when he did not, he reportedly said publicly that the center did not have what it took to label the Kumasi-based center as the Ghana National Cultural Center. Therefore, as the Emeritus Prelate disclosed with irritation, the official directed that the center he had just visited should be known as the Kumasi Cultural Center because the military regime was going to encourage the establishment other regional cultural centers.

As a fellow Oxford-educated Ghanaian, the Emeritus Archbishop's reaction to the utterances of the military regime's cultural leader was understandable; in essence, he detected ingratitude on the part of the new regime, compared to how the late President Nkrumah, upon his similarly brief visit to Kumasi, embraced the center's work and agreed to provide assistance to its founder, Dr. Kyerematen, and everything fell into place accordingly.

ALIGNMENT WITH OTHER CULTURAL GIANTS IN GHANAIAN HISTORY: GHANA PRIME MINISTER K.A. BUSIA AND DR. KYEREMATEN

Meanwhile, a much older Oxford graduate, who shared similar cultural and ethnic aspirations with Dr. Kyerematen, was the late Ghana prime minister Kofi Busia, who was born in 1913, indeed three years before Dr. Kyerematen, was known to have been born into a Wenchi royal family in today's Brong Ahafo Region; it was very much like Dr. Kyerematen, who also had royal family background from Patase, near Kumasi. Both graduates of Oxford belonged to Ghana's dominant Akan ethnic group. At his birth, the Ahafo area was part of the Ashanti R Region of the Gold Coast, and was said to be the hunting ground for the *Asantehene* (King of Ashanti). Like Dr. Quaison-Sackey, he also attended Mfatsipim Secondary School in Cape Coast, in today's Central Region of Ghana, an institution that is similar in quality to Adisadel College.

After earning a first class (*summa cum laude*) degree in medieval and modern history from the University of London, Busia became a teacher—just like Dr. Kyerematen—before he entered the University of Oxford's University College to earn a degree in philosophy, politics and economics (the famous PPE sequence). However, his doctoral (D.Phil.) degree in social anthropology was earned in 1947, with a dissertation that was titled, "The Position of the Chief in the Modern Political System of Ashanti: A Study of the Influence of Contemporary Social Changes on Ashanti Political Institutions." Several contemporary African students and British scholars, who knew Dr. Busia at Oxford, often joked that since it was a lot more fashionable to say that one studied sociology, as opposed to social anthropology, Dr. Busia did not bother to stress that he studied that subject, although he was never dishonest about his credentials. As a fellow Akan, with strong Ashanti roots, Dr. Busia harbored identical cultural aspirations with Dr. Kyerematen. Indeed, that was why they studied several aspects of Akan royalty, with an emphasis on the Ashantis. It was, in fact, not surprising that both of them wrote theses with Ashanti cultural themes.

It was in 1969 that Dr. Busia was inaugurated as Ghana's new Prime Minister. That, indeed, was after the post-1966 Nkrumah overthrow. Dr. Kyerematen, in fact, had been invited to serve as the Secretary for local Government by the post-1966 military regime, which was—at the time—headed by the then Lt.-General A.A. Afrifa, one of the principal coup leaders, who attended Adisadel College like Dr. Kyerematen. The feeling among several Akan leaders in Ghana, at the time, was that the Busia regime in Ghana would continue to assist Dr. Kyerematen and his cultural center, but that did not happen.

What was interesting was that, as a fellow Akan, Dr. Busia did appreciate the cultural importance of Dr. Kyerematen's Kumasi-based center. However, his political nemesis—the late President Nkrumah—had earlier extended assistance to the center and its founder, which was accepted by Dr. Kyerematen. Therefore, as suspected by several observers, the late Prime Minister Busia did not offer anything, a scenario that did not surprise many astute politicians. Also, it was not publicly known that when foreign dignitaries visited Ghana, as the guests of the Party government of Dr. Busia, efforts were never made to add visits to the center. In addition to benefitting from the advocacy of others, Dr. A.A.Y. Kyerematen and the centre that he worked hard to establish was engaged by giants of African politics and scholarship in interesting ways.

DISSEMINATING THE WORK
OF CULTURAL LEGENDS:
DR. WILLIE ABRAHAM AND DR. KYEREMATEN

Another Ghanaian with Oxford credentials, who showed an interest in the work of Dr. Kyerematen and his cultural center in Ghana, is retired Philosophy Professor William (Willie) Abraham. Like Dr. Kyerematen and others, he also attended the Cape Coast-based Adisadel College. Born in 1934, he went to the United Kingdom to study philosophy at University of Oxford, after he earned a first-class bachelor of arts degree in philosophy from the University of Ghana the very year of Ghana's independence (1957). He continued an advanced study of philosophy at All Souls College of the University of Oxford, where he served as a fellow before leaving to work at for University of London's School of Oriental and African Studies (SOAS) in 1960. Two years later (in 1962) he returned to University of Ghana, when his friend, the late President Kwame Nkrumah was the Head of State.

A prolific scholar like Dr. Kyerematen, his older Oxford alumnus, Professor Abraham published a seminal philosophy book titled, *The Mind of Africa*. Apart from being elected vice-president of the Ghana Academy of Sciences in 1963, he went on to succeed Conor Cruise O'Brien as the Vice-Chancellor of University of Ghana in September of 1965. At the time, he was known to be very close to then President Nkrumah. The suspicion was that, as a philosopher, he played roles in the philosophical books that Nkrumah wrote while in office, including *Consciencism*.

Dr. Abraham, who is in retirement as a philosophy professor, also admired Dr. Kyerematen for his famous cultural center, which brought a lot of fame to Ghana as a cultural mecca. As a fellow graduate of Adisadel College, Professor Abraham was known by observers of Ghana politics to have played roles in encouraging the late President Nkrumah to extend assistance to Dr. Kyerematen and his center.

Apart from *Consciencism*, as a book with a philosophical theme, Professor Abraham was also suspected by critics of President Nkrumah to know about the writing of the very controversial book by Nkrumah titled, *Neo-Colonialism: The Last Stage of Imperialism*, published in 1965 by the British publishing company, Thomas Nelson and Sons of London. Some of these famous books and others were launched at the Ghana National Cultural Centre that Dr. Kyerematen established and headed. Such book launchings, a very regular occurrence for several authors, were attended by many Ghanaian scholars and students. There are rumors that Western intelligence agencies, including the Central Intelligence Agency of the United States, were prompted to work for the overthrow of the Ghana regime headed by Nkrumah mainly because of this book, which castigated capitalism and put socialism on a pedestal.

PROFESSORS ADU BOAHEN, ALI A. MAZRUI AND DR. KYEREMATEN

In fact, an Oxford scholar who equally appreciated Dr. Kyerematen's cultural interests and expertise was Professor Ali A. Mazrui, also a much younger fellow graduate. Born on February 21, 1933, Dr. Mazrui was 17 years younger than Dr. Kyerematen. He earned his doctoral (D.Phil.) degree from Nuffield College of the University of Oxford in 1966. While Dr. Kyerematen and his cultural center were seen as beneficiaries of then President Nkrumah's monetary largesse, Professor Mazrui, who passed away in his prime as an astute scholar, is reputed to have been influenced by President Nkrumah's firebrand Pan-Africanist idealism, including his book titled *Consciencism*. Indeed, it is believed by some Pan-Africanist scholars that it was ideas advanced by Nkrumaism that prompted Dr. Mazrui's notion of Africa's Triple Heritage, which he named as Africanity, Islam and Christianity. Professor Mazrui, however, chuckled at this insinuation, for at the time Nkrumah was overthrown in 1966, he was a professor of political science at Makerere University in Uganda, where *Transition Magazine* was based. In fact, he wrote a very critical assessment of the deposed Ghanaian leader and his ideological underpinnings, which was famously titled as: "Kwame Nkrumah: Leninist Czar."

PROFESSOR ALBERT ADU BOAHEN
AND DR. KYEREMATEN

It was Professor Albert Adu Boahen, who, reportedly, introduced Professor
Mazrui to Dr. Keyerematen and his growing creation known, at the time, as
the then Kumasi Cultural Centre, before it was renamed as Ghana National
Cultural Centre on the advice or prompting of the late President Nkrumah.
In a discussion about the subject, Professor Mazrui, who had a razor-sharp
mind, remembered that after the 1966 *coup d'état* in Ghana, the new National
Liberation Council (NLC) government also encouraged Dr. Kyerematen to
change the center's name from the Ghana National Cultural Centre to Centre
for National Culture, which was a way of making sure that the name was
in harmony with other similar centers that had mushroomed throughout the
regions of Ghana.

When Professor Mazrui first visited the center in the early 1970s, in the
company of Professor Boahen, the eminent historian, he said that it reminded
him of various places, including a couple of well-kept museums he had
seen in Europe. His remarks were a way of lauding what Dr. Kyerematen
was doing in Ghana as far as culture was concerned. He was happy that he
could buy from sellers at the center several Ghanaian handicrafts, including
carvings and hand-woven Kente cloth, all of which he purchased as gifts for
friends and his own family back home.

Dr. Mazrui, the prolific Kenyan author, intimated to Professor Assensoh:
"I was overly awed, A. B., when I met the founder of the centre, my fellow
Oxon [Dr. Kyerematen]." He then talked at length with Dr. Kyerematen and
realized that he was at a lecture given by the Ghanaian icon about African
culture at the Africa Centre in London, not far from Trafalgar Square and its
tourist attractions. They also discussed several aspects of their student years
at the University of Oxford and its unlimited opportunities.

It was, in fact, on advice from Dr. Kyerematen's tremendous cultural expe-
rience and appeal that caused several international scholars to be bestowed
with Ghanaian traditional titles by chiefs and other local leaders. The his-
tory Professor Boahen, just as prolific as Dr. Kyerematen, recommended Dr.
Mazrui to be enstooled as the honorary Akan chieftain, with the title of *Nana*.
Professor Adu Boahen was well placed to plead for this title for Professor
Mazrui, for he had similar traditional and intellectual links to those of Dr.
Kyerematen and Dr. Busia, who promoted Akan culture through history. In
fact, as his biographical information indicated, he was born in Oseim, Eastern
Ghana, on May 24, 1932, to Presbyterian parents, although Professor Boahen
traced his ancestral roots to Juaben in the Ashanti Region of Ghana, hence
was given a royal burial there when he died in 2006.

Professor Boahen, like Dr. Kyerematen and other older Ghanaian intellectuals before him, attended state and local religious elementary schools (between 1938 and 1947) before he subsequently attended Mfantsipim School in Cape Coast, Professor Boahen studied History at the University College of then Gold Coast at Legon, which is now University of Ghana. Upon earning his first degree in 1956 (awarded through University of London, with honors in history), he received his Ph.D. in African history from the School of Oriental and African Studies of the University of London in 1959.

DR. J.B. DANQUAH AND DR. KYEREMATEN

Also, it is a known fact that Dr. Joseph Boakye ("J.B.") Danquah, a leading political leader and a distinguished Jurist, earned his undergraduate and post-graduate degrees from University of London in Law. Although much older than Dr. Kyerematen and the others, it is important to provide an anecdotal fact that Dr. Danquah, in 1922, entered the University College of London as a philosophy student. Upon earning his bachelor of arts (B.A.) degree in 1925, he excelled by winning the John Stuart Mill Scholarship in the Philosophy of Mind and Logic. He subsequently began his doctor of philosophy degree, which he earned in two years, with his dissertation titled, "The Moral End as Moral Excellence." In fact, he was the first West African citizen to earn the doctor of philosophy (Ph.D.) degree from any British university. As he was working on his doctoral dissertation in London, Danquah entered the Inner Temple (an Inns of Court), and he was called to the English Bar in 1926. Just like the late President Nkrumah, former Foreign Minister Ako Adjei and others in London, Dr. Danquah also took time off his studies to get involved in African student politics. He also edited a publication for the West African Students' Union (WASU), and he eventually became the president of the Union.

Like Dr. Busia, Dr. Boahen and others, Dr. Kyerematen spent some time at the University of Ghana, in his case as a fellow of the Institute of African Studies. However, Dr. Boahen spent his entire professional career at Ghana's premier university, as he was first employed at the University of Ghana in 1959. Between 1971 and his retirement in 1990, he was a full professor, becoming an emeritus professor at his retirement. In his active professorial years, he chaired the Department of History at University of Ghana from 1967 to 1975, as the first African scholar to do so, as well as serving as a Dean from 1973 to 1975. A noted historian, Professor Adu Boahen served on the editorial board of the *Journal of African History*, published by Cambridge University Press. Apart from serving in fellowship positions overseas, sometimes as a visiting scholar at such foreign universities as Australia National

University (1969), Columbia University in New York (1970), and State University of New York (SUNY, 1991), Professor Boahen like Professor Mazrui, worked between 1993 and 1999 for UNESCO's scholarly and expert committee, which published UNESCO's *General History of Africa* reference books in eight volumes.

In fact, upon Professor Boahen's death in May 2006, Ghanaian writer Ivor Agyeman-Duah, who authored the widely acclaimed biography of Ghana's President John Agyekum Kufuor, wrote in *The Guardian* newspaper of London that Professor Boahen, who had died at age 74, dared to give an anti-military lecture at the British Council Hall in Accra, Ghana, during the 1982–1992 military regime that was ruled by the late Flight Lieutenant Jerry John Rawlings. However, to the credit of the Rawlings' regime, the history professor emeritus was not arrested as feared, not even after he had ended his address with a quotation from James Baldwin's book, *The Fire Next Time*, invoking the possibility of the Ghanaian military either being devoured by itself, or even being overthrown by civil disobedience. The revised version of Professor Boahen's lecture was published in 1998 as *The Ghanaian Sphinx: The Contemporary History of Ghana 1972–1987* (Agyeman-Duah, 2006: obituary). While many argue that Dr. Kyerematen did his best to stay out of the political fray, as the next chapter will show, he did engage in politics when it was necessary to safeguard the work and future of the Cultural Centre.

Chapter 4

De-Centering Politics

Dr. Kyerematen's Political Maneuvering as Part of the NLC Military Administration (1966–1969)

In the immediate years following the Second World War [WWII], the British Empire entered a period of social and political agitation. The initial plan of gradually introducing self-government into its vast overseas territories was abandoned as many forces of change swept across its wide-flung parts. British Africa was not left out of this unfolding drama, as it experienced a fair share of bloody, chaotic, and sometimes nonviolent upheavals. In the comparatively small British colony of the Gold Coast, the upheaval was sudden and dramatic but relatively orderly. The historiography on the independence movement in the Gold Coast in the 1940s is impressive and voluminous. Most of it focuses on individuals such as Kwame Nkrumah and J.B. Danquah, and their contributions to and roles within emergent political parties, such as the United Gold Coast Convention. There were, in most cases, members of the United Gold Coast Convention (UGCC) and Convention People's Party (CPP) (Sarpong, 2016: 89).

Dr. Alexander Atta Yaw (A.A.Y.) Kyerematen—who returned from his British academic sojourn to the then British colony of the Gold Coast (which became Ghana in 1957 upon its independence)—was very much aware of the turbulent nature of the social and political scene, which is very well captured in the facts above from Dr. Nana Yaw B. Sarpong's very apt published chapter, "Framing Contentious Politics in the Gold Coast" in *Kwame Nkrumah, 1909–1972: A Controversial African Visionary* (Lundt and Marx, 2016). After all, Dr. Sarpong has demonstrated in his publication that the historiography on the independence movement was very vast, and therefore Dr. Kyerematen, as studious as he was, obtained copies of the available publications to read.

It was, therefore, not very surprising that the future Dr. Kyerematen, like his many young citizens of Ghana, liked the intrigue of his country's politics, but he did loath partisan or soap-box politics. Instead, he was willing to offer free advice to aspiring politicians and professionals. Former Ghana President John Agyekum Kufuor put it best in his provided foreword to this publication in the following words:

> Dr. Kyerematen was also interested in politics, yet with the background that he had, he would not be the soap-box or platform one; instead, he intended to use the power of politics for cultural development of Ghanaian society. (Kufuor, see foreword)

As further explained by Oxford-educated ex-President Kufuor, Dr. Kyerematen did offer him free advice on what constituency to adopt for Kufuor's parliamentary politics (either Subin or Atwima Nwabiagya), and that was, indeed, how far the cultural prince went, no more and no less. However, he was so accurate in predicting success for the young political aspirant that, in the end, then Lawyer Kufuor contested successfully and won the Atwima Nwabiagya constituency to enter the Parliament of Ghana's Second Republic, with Oxford-educated Professor Kofi Abrefa Busia as the Prime Minister with executive powers, while fellow Oxford-educated Lawyer Edward Akufo-Addo—father of Ghana's current President Nana Akufo-Addo—was the titular President. The future President Kufuor, at the time, was initially appointed Deputy Foreign Minister of Ghana.

DR. KYEREMATEN AND THE NEW GHANA
POLITICS UNDER THEN PRESIDENT NKRUMAH

Eventually, Nkrumah emerged victorious in his post-independent Ghana politics, but several intellectuals were skeptical of the prevailing political climate. While many of them—including Drs. J.B. Danquah, K.A. Busia and others—openly detested what was going on politically. However, Dr. Kyerematen, who was very close to several major Ashanti Chiefs and the King (*Asantehene*) did not openly show any hostility toward the Convention People's Party (CPP) regime of Nkrumah. It was, therefore, not unusual that the Oxbridge-trained Cultural Anthropologist (Dr. Kyerematen) succeeded with his project, the initial Kumasi Cultural Center.

Although Dr. Kyerematen later accepted wise counsel from the reigning Asantehene, Otumfuo Sir Osei Tutu Agyeman Prempeh II, and others to accept governmental assistance, hence then President Nkrumah came to his aid, as earlier reported, it was also a fact that he did not show any practical interest in the partisan politics of the day. There were, indeed, many reasons for his attitude.

In *Kwame Nkrumah As I Knew Him*, Genoveva Marais—who after the 1966 Ghana *coup d'état* moved to Sierra Leone and became Mrs. Genoveva Marais-Kanu, upon marrying Sierra Leonean Victor S. Kanu—catalogued part of the chilling political climate in Ghana, which did not make politics very appealing to someone like Dr. Kyerematen. The unpleasant atmosphere and other reasons, according to Marais of South African citizenship, made the Ghanaian leader "plan to isolate himself from the public, if he were to get things done." (Marais, 1972: 116–117; Assensoh, 1998: 109).

Of course, Dr. Kyerematen was correct to stay away from the partisan politics. After all, Marais went on to add that upon becoming isolated, then President Nkrumah antagonized the very people, who should have understood his position, as they reportedly felt slighted. In the end, as further revealed by the female confidante of Nkrumah, his long-time political allies abandoned him simply because they no longer had empathy for him. (Marais, 1972: 117; Assensoh, 1998: 109).

Meanwhile, ex-President Nkrumah also became unpopular due to some of his political policies, including the introduction in 1958 of the Preventive Detention Act (PDA), under which several of his political opponents—including the legal luminary and former financial benefactor, Dr. J.B. Danquah—were detained without proper legal adjudication, or with no charges brought against them for trial or conviction. Marais seemed to justify some of the policies, as she disclosed in 1972, that "there were frequent plots to overthrow Nkrumah and that the earliest of these was carried out on November 20, 1958, when R.R. Amponsah and a Major Awhaitey [allegedly] teamed up with others to seize Nkrumah, some of his cabinet, and then carry out a *coup d'état*." (Marais, 1972: 118–124; Assensoh, 1998: 109–110).

Unfortunately, Nkrumah' ideological stance, enveloped in aspects of socialism and even communism, did not appeal well to his opponents, who included conservative Oxford-educated Busia and others. That was confirmed by scholars, who pointed out some of the left-wing influences on the Ghanaian leader. For example, Dr. Sapong, *inter alia*, wrote: "Apart from learning organizational techniques, Nkrumah sought theoretical ways by which the colonial question and imperialism might be solved. This led him to closely study Hagel, Marx, Engels, Lenin, Mzzini, and Garvey their writings greatly influenced him." (Sapong, 2016: 101).

With his mostly British education, up to his studies at Oxford and later Cambridge, Dr. Kyerematen, like several other Western-educated Ghanaians, could not mortgage his intellectual freedom for what the late President Nkrumah was preaching.

DR. KYEREMATEN EMBRACES THE MILITARY
POLITICS OF THE POST-1966 NLC

Then President Nkrumah stubbornly believed that a new ideological system would suit Ghana that he was leading a lot more, hence he asserted that even a system based on social justice and a democratic constitution could be lacking after attaining independence, including measures of a totalitarian kind. He added that in doing so, African leaders in such nations as Ghana, Tanzania, Kenya and other countries must find an ideology that is beneficial to their citizenry while also not alienating to pro-capitalist interests in the various nations. The contradiction with Nkrumah was that although he had socialistic interests, he saw the need to secure Western financial assistance for his major developmental projects, including Ghana's hydro-electric project on the Volta River; however, his stubborn claim was that Ghana needed socialism to carry out his programs (Assensoh, 1989: 203–204). However, Dr. Kyerematen and several Western educated Ghanaians could not tolerate the socialist rhetoric, although unlike the others, Dr. Kyerematen was very quiet about it.

The opportune moment came on February 24, 1966, when the Ghana Armed Forces teamed up with the police, under the leadership of Kumasi-based Second Infantry Brigade Colonel (later promoted full General) Emmanuel K. Kotoka overthrew the Nkrumah government on that day. The announcement accompanying the military-*cum*-police seizure of power explained that "their action was to save Ghana from Nkrumah's rampant economic mismanagement." (Assensoh, 1998: 112).

Upon seizing power from Nkrumah's elected CPP government, while he was on a peace trip to Vietnam, the new ruling class, the National Liberation Council (NLC) realized that it needed well-educated technocrats and specialists to be recruited for national service. That was how the late Lt.-General Akwasi Amankwah ("A.A.") Afrifa, as the then Chairman of the ruing NLC, saw the need to invite Dr. Kyerematen, his fellow Adisadel College-educated Ghanaian, to join the cabinet as the Secretary for Local Government.

Many observers have noted that Dr. Kyerematen, whose National Cultural Center benefitted from Nkrumah's government with an annual monetary grant, indeed a subvention of sorts, was not merely biting the finger, which fed his center. Instead, many meaningful Ghanaians and observers simply saw the deep nationalism, which motivated him to accept the NLC's invitation to join the cabinet. In fact, the Catholic Church's Emeritus Archbishop Peter Akwasi Sarpong, a fellow Oxford-educated Anthropologist, expressed a similar sentiment in an elaborate interview we had with him for this book.

"My dear friend, Alex, did not embrace the NLC out of either greed or opportunism. Instead, he did so out of national service. After all, he did not need them at that stage of his very successful life," Emeritus Archbishop Sarpong emphasized.

Speaking from a wealth of seasoned experience as an intellectual and a dedicated citizen of Ghana, the retired Catholic prelate—who also served on the Governing Council of the Kumasi-based Kwame Nkrumah University of Science and Technology (KNUST)—went on to elaborate that without such very seasoned administrative experiences of someone like Dr. Kyerematen in the NLC cabinet, there would have been a lot of bloodshed in the street committed by the military, compared to what Ghanaians experienced when the late President Jerry John Rawlings led his first *coup d'état.*

GHANA, THE ARMED FORCES
REVOLUTIONARY COUNCIL (AFRC), FROM
JUNE 4, 1979, TO SEPTEMBER 24, 1979

When Emeritus Archbishop Sarpong spoke, it did remind us—as interviewers—that six Generals of the Ghana Armed Forces, including two former Heads of State, were executed by the Armed Forces Revolutionary Council (AFRC) by firing squad under the former President Rawlings. As reported by the news media, the regime of the late Flt. Lt. Rawlings condemned the Generals to death, allegedly, over claims of cleansing the country of corruption. Sadly, the two Heads of State—Lieutenant-General Okatakyie Akwasi Amankwa Afrifa (Head of State from 1968 to 1969) and General Fred William Kwasi Akuffo (also, Head of State from 1978 to 1979)—were shot in public by a firing squad at the Teshie Army Shooting Range in the country's capital, Accra. Also, executed with the Generals were former Navy Commander Rear Admiral Joy Amedume; former Air Force Commander, Air Vice-Marshal George Yaw Boakye; Deputy Head of State and former Chief of Defence Staff, Major-General Robert Ebenezer Abosey Kotei, all of these officers were members of the erstwhile Supreme Military Council (SMC). The only non-SMC member, executed was then Foreign Affairs Commissioner Colonel Roger Felli, allegedly selected to be executed to meet a geographic regional distribution quota among the executed officers.

In line with the way the retired Catholic prelate saw the moribund political scene of Ghana, which benefited tremendously from Dr. Kyerematen's willingness to serve the NLC in order to ensure stability and calm, former Ghana President Kufuor—who wrote the foreword to this book—lamented in a statement—when meeting widows and family members of the executed Generals—that the six Generals "were unjustly murdered." As a trained and practicing Lawyer, then President Kufuor lamented further the fact that the executed officers "were not tried in a court of law and found guilty to suffer punishment prescribed by law."

Meanwhile, to soothe the bereaved families, the government of President Kufuor agreed for the exhumation of the bodies of the buried officers and handed over to their families for proper burial. To help heal Ghana from the pains of the execution and other extra-judicial actions of the military regimes, including the unjust executions, then President Kufuor disclosed that he had set up a Reconciliation Commission "to try to heal the hurts and wounds within our community so that there will be peace for governance."

Chapter 5

Dr. Kyerematen's Impact on Ghana through National Services

"Dr. Kyerematen's many books on Ghana's cultural heritage do not only teach the younger generation the cultural aspirations of their forefathers but also educate them on the need to treasure and practice the life and thinking of their ancestors. Indeed, we have lost a great one, but we hope [that] his work and ideas will continue to live with us and become a shining symbol for the future generation to emulate," said Otumfuo Opoku Ware II, Asantehene.

—Public Tribute by the Ashanti King

The words, quoted above, were part of the tribute that the occupier of Ashanti people's Golden Stool in 1976 (Otumfuo Opoku Ware II) expressed as part of his much longer public expression honoring Dr. Kyerematen in death. It showed that mainstream scholars were not the only ones who saw the intellect of Dr. Kyerematen but custodians of Ghanaian cultures and traditions as well. His fellow Adisadel College alumnus, Dr. Robert Gardiner, spoke eloquently by stressing his selfless nature as well. Apart from serving as executive director of the United Nation's Economic Commission for Africa (ECA) in Addis Ababa, Ethiopia, Dr. Gardiner was a former Commissioner for Economic Planning and the leader of the Ghana government's delegation to the burial of Dr. Kyerematen. Among other laudable details, Dr. Gardner noted: "Alex, as I knew him, from Adisadel College till he died, was a man who always worked to edify the nation, and not himself. He was in a situation [in which] he could have amassed wealth. But he died not a wealthy man. He did not work for money."

Although Mrs. Peggy Appiah was from a famous English family in the United Kingdom, she also recognized the high stature of the Kyerematens, as their families lived not far from each other in Kumasi, the Ashanti capital of Ghana. The city, where Dr. Kyerematen acquired land from the Ashanti royal family to establish his famous cultural centre, is so picturesque that it is nicknamed by many Ghanaians and other Africans as the Garden City of West Africa. Therefore, the famous author seized the opportunity to produce a six-stanza poem as a tribute in Dr. Kyerematen's memory. Mrs. Peggy Appiah's poem, in full, read:

> For surely his works shall live after him.
> Weep then, O people of Ghana,
> A branch from the [mighty] tree has fallen,
> Mighty the branch and fruitful,
> Yet has it fallen.
> Weep then, but listen!
> Hear the wind whispering
> In young trees Springing From seed he has sown.
> Their roots grown deep,
> Deep in the land of their fathers; Listen and hear.
> Surely, the drums are playing,
> The long horn and the short,
> The *gongong*,
> The beat of feet drumming Praise to this son of Ghana
> For surely his works shall live after him.
> So does the star in the wide sky shining
> Reflect in the waters,
> In still pool and stream;
> Spreading its light to far horizons,
> Myriad sparklets gleaming.
> So does the worth of one man
> And his devotion
> Guide as a light,
> Lead to further glory,
> One man his God serving Stand for us all.
> Rejoice then, and weep not,
> Still his light following:
> He who loves all, loses not
> Is at one with his Master. (Peggy Appiah, pp. 20–21)

The center's then Director S. F. Adjei, who had succeeded Dr. Kyerematen, also wrote another poetic tribute, which was titled, "A Tribute in Memory of Dr. Kyerematen." In it, he traced his humble beginnings as a student of Adisadel College; he added in his tribute that Dr. Kyerematen and his school mates played a role in constructing some of the buildings at the present site of Adisadel College at Cape Coast. Referring to Dr. Kyerematen as "Father of Festivals," Director Adjei, who felt humbled in the presence of his late boss, ended his very touching poetic obituary: "May the light you lit continue to shine in the Hearts and Minds of the present and future Generations and Generations yet unborn. A crusader for cultural revival in Ghana," (S. F. Adjei, p. 24).

Among other distinguished individuals praising Dr. Kyerematen were governing council members of the Kwame Nkrumah University of Science and Technology (KNUST), which he had served actively for many years, including as chairman. For example, KNUST Vice-Chancellor E. Evans-Anfom, who was to later head the West African Examinations Council, WAEC, published a tribute in a news write-up (included in the appendix). Reporter Daniel Appiah-Adjei wrote that Nana Brefo Boateng—who is from Jamasi, Ashanti, and is a former director of the Centre for National Culture, Kumasi—urged "The powers there be" to name the cultural center after Dr. Alexander Atta Yaw Kyerematen, the founder and the first director.

Nana Boateng made his statement during the Kwame Nkrumah Centenary Lectures organized by the Cultural Initiatives Support Programme (CISP), under the auspices of the National Commission on Culture and funded by the European Development Fund (EDF). The event was held on Wednesday, 30th September, 2009, at the Centre for National Culture in Kumasi. This lecture was chaired by Oheneba Adusei Poku, Akyempemhene.

As it is discussed in the appendix, several meaningful Ghanaians have suggested, since Dr. Kyerematen's death in 1976, that the National Cultural Centre should be named in his honor. Among those clamoring for the honor is former centre director Brefo-Sarpong of Jamasi, Ashanti. In his opinion, Dr. Kyerematen has done so much for cultural awareness in Ghana in general and, in particular, for the center that he should be so honored. However, in our interview with Catholic Archbishop Emeritus Sarpong, he explained that it would certainly be a befitting tribute to name the center after Dr. Kyerematen, but that he knew Dr. Kyerematen so well that, were he alive, Kyerematen would never have accepted such an elaborate honor. "Look, Dr. Kyerematen was a very humble citizen and man of God, who was not given to ostentation. That is why I feel very strongly that he would not accept that sort of high honor. I may be wrong," he added during the interview.

As we have also pointed out elsewhere, both the Archbishop Emeritus (whose brief profile is in the appendix section) and Dr. Kyerematen shared varied circumstances, including the fact that they were graduates of the University of Oxford. However, they attended different colleges. They also served together, for several years, on the Governing Council of Kwame Nkrumah University of Science and Technology (KNUST) in Kumasi. Therefore, from his tribute, upon Dr. Kyerematen's death in 1976, Most Rev. Bishop Sarpong observed that, "no one could come into close and intimate contact with Dr. Kyerematen, as I had the privilege to do, without being struck and impressed by his extraordinary devotion to duty, unparalleled simplicity of life, amazing spirit of sacrifice, exceptional religiosity, genuine friendliness and, above all, his deep commitment to the course of culture. His remarkable life, is a life worth talking about and emulating." The Anglican Bishop of Kumasi at the time, the Rt. Rev. J. B. Arthur, presided over a memorial and thanksgiving service at St. Cyprian's Anglican Cathedral, on Sunday, December 5, 1976, at 9:00 a.m. This was followed by a Requiem Mass at the National Cultural Centre, Kumasi, on Monday, December 6, 1976. From Bishop Arthur's tribute is the following edifying quotation: "Alex showed a rare talent for organization. His life was a shining example to the contemporary intellectual who, in a world of bribery and corrupt practices, is called upon to exercise the highest integrity and render devoted and loyal services to the nation."

In fact, co-author A. B. Assensoh served in the early 1970s as deputy editor of the Kumasi-based newspaper, *The Pioneer*, which often wrote critical editorials about governments and their officials. Consequently, in 1972, the National Redemption Council (NRC) of the executed head of state, General Ignatius Kutu Acheampong, banned the newspaper when it questioned suspected corruption in military and police ranks at the time. The editorial's refrain, in the form of a question, explored whether or not corruption was still rife in public life in Ghana, a query that irritated Acheampong and his military council leadership (Assensoh, 2018).

The Pioneer newspaper, published by Abura Printing Press, which produced the December 5, 1976, program used for Dr. Kyerematen's memorial and thanksgiving service, praised him as a person with great nobility. In a November 1976 editorial, the editor of *The Pioneer* wrote (as quoted in the funeral program): "[Dr. Kyerematen] has left one indelible mark on the sands of time with the introduction of the Annual National Festival of Arts, which he instituted in 1956."

From our research for this book, we learned from several former and current employees of the National Cultural Center how Dr. Kyerematen was seen as a father and uncle figure, so was overwhelmingly called *Wofa* (in Ashanti, i.e., Uncle) by all and sundry. Former directors of the Centre, who followed his leadership, have spoken eloquently in his honor and, in fact, some of them have echoed the need for the National Cultural Centre to be renamed in honor of this illustrious son of Ghana. They included Dr. E. Osei Kofi, Nana Brefo Boateng, Owusu Akyaw, and, the current Director, S. F. Adjei, a product of the famous T. I. Ahmadiyya Secondary School in Kumasi and the University of Ghana. Below is an excerpt from Dr. Osei Kofi's tribute:

> We owe Dr. Kyerematen an everlasting debt of gratitude for the light he lit for us. This light would remain a source of inspiration to Ghanaians as a whole

and to all mankind, who are concerned with the uplifting of culture. Although he is no more with us, his soul goes marching on because, as people flock to *Anokyekrom* at the Ghana National Cultural Centre every Saturday and to the Kumasi Zoo, they would be coming in regular contact with the spirit of Dr. Kyerematen.

Dr. Kyerematen's exemplary life leaves us with little surprise when his mourners saw Catholic and Anglican church leaders come together with other religious leaders to honor him. After all, in his writings, he did not shy away from pointing out Christian traits in the characters of traditional and other leaders. For example, in *Daasebre Sir Osei Tutu Agyeman Prempeh II, Asantehene*, Dr. Kyerematen made sure to point out the Christian fact about the Asantehene, who happened to have reigned 39 years, indeed much longer than any other Asantehene before him, including even Nana Obiri Yeboah, who had earlier reigned for thirty-four years (1663–1697). In his own Christian way, Dr. Kyerematen made sure to point out that "if anyone asked [Otumfuo Nana Sir Osei Tutu Agyeman Prempeh II] what was the secret of the successes during his thirty-nine years' reign, he would reply that it was due to his reliance on the Holy Bible. "If [the person] was fortunate, [the Asantehene] would produce the Bible presented to him by Rev. Mr. Addo, a Methodist pastor, on the day of his enstoolment" (p. 7). Due to the constant use of that Bible, Dr. Kyerematen further wrote that "[the Bible] has now been reduced to a threadbare of a Bible, apparently through its constant use. [Asantehene's] devotion and deep trust in God is sometimes frightening. (p. 7)

THE KYEREMATEN LECTURES

By 1990, it had been almost two decades since Dr. Alexander Atta Yaw Kyerematen died in 1976, and it was in that year that the National Cultural Centre that he conceived and established instituted the Kyerematen Memorial Lectures, a series of lectures to be given by prominent personalities to honor his memory and legacy. That was so because when alive, Dr. Kyerematen eschewed ostentation and anything that sought to either promote him personally or to heap praises on what he had created. Indeed, many knew him as a man of great modesty and humility.

The foregoing factors were underscored very vividly when we interviewed Catholic Archbishop Emeritus Peter Kwasi Sarpong of Kumasi for this publication. He pointed out that when alive, several men and women of substance endeavored to name the centre after its creator, but Dr. Kyerematen never wanted to hear of such suggestions. It also became a familiar refrain, he added, since he died in 1976. "I knew Alex very well; he was not about self-adulation or promotion. He won't go for that at all," Archbishop Emeritus Sarpong added.

For the memorial lecture series, the first lecture was given by Dr. Mohammed Ben Abdallah, a very well-known Ghanaian playwright, who once headed the School of Performing Arts at University of Ghana. At the time, he held the cabinet-level position that was responsible for culture in Ghana. Therefore, he used his lecture to announce the cultural policy of the Provisional National Defence Council (PNDC), which had Flt. Lt. Jerry John Rawlings as head of state of Ghana.

In his inaugural lecture, titled "The Role of Cultural Centers in National Development: A Case Study of the Cultural Center in Kumasi," Ghana-based Centre for Intellectual Renewal Director Ivor Agyeman-Duah, in a published pamphlet, quoted him as "spelling out the then [PNDC] Government's National Cultural Policy and the expected functions of the Centre for National Culture as well as the emanating of district cultural centres from them" (Agyeman-Duah, 1995, p. ix). He expanded the policy to explain further that its two main functions were to: "(a) implement and monitor Government policies relating to the development, promotion, preservation and appreciation of culture and the arts in the region; [and] (b) identify, organize and mobilize the artistic resource of the regions and develop the commercial potential of such resources" (Agyeman-Duah, 1995, p. ix).

By implication, Dr. Abdallah was informing Ghanaians that the PNDC military government would, henceforth, see Dr. Kyerematen's Kumasi-based National Cultural Centre only as the Centre for National Culture in Kumasi, but not as the sole centre that would deal with cultural issues in Ghana. He made that known, as his office was to ensure that several similar centres of culture were to be established in all of the remaining nine regional capitals of Ghana's ten regions. He also announced that even various Ghanaian districts were to have their own district-level cultural centers. In his opinion, the regions, with their large populations, coupled with their various districts, were ready to move along the cultural policy path of the ruling Provisional National Defence Council (PNDC). Shown below is a listing of all of the ten regions of Ghana as well as their capitals, and, as announced by Ghana's 2010 population census, the growing national population:

In spite of the new national cultural policy, which seemed to critics of the PNDC regime to be a deliberate effort of Dr. Abdallah and the PNDC regime to try to undermine Dr. Kyerematen's widely praised efforts in the area of Ghanaian culture, Director Agyeman-Duah introduced his pamphlet with a one-paragraph quotation from a long 1976 obituary that was published in a local Ghanaian newspaper. Among other details, he wrote: "In an obituary article published after Dr. Alexander Atta Yaw Kyerematen's death in 1976, the writer wrote: 'The Ghana National Cultural Centre stands as [an] everlasting memorial to his name. Conceived and built under his untiring leadership and supervision, the centre will remain a perpetual testimony to the

Table 5.1. Ten Regions of Republic of Ghana and Their Capital Towns. Courtesy of the authors. Created by Dr. Augustine Adu Frimpong.

Region	Capital	Area (km²)	Population*
Ashanti	Kumasi	24,889	4,780,380
Brong-Ahafo	Sunyani	39,557	2,310,983
Greater Accra	Accra	3,245	4,010,054
Central	Cape Coast	9,826	2,201,863
Eastern	Koforidua	19,323	2,633,154
Northern	Tamale	70,384	2,479,461
Western	Sekondi-Takoradi	23,921	2,376,021
Upper East	Bolgatanga	8,842	1,046,545
Upper West	Wa	18,476	702,110
Volta	Ho	20,570	2,118,252

strength of his will and the tenacity with which he pursued his convictions'" (Agyeman-Duah,1995).

In his view, however, Dr. Abdallah, as the cultural guru under the PNDC military regime, felt that, as he explained in the inaugural lecture, the Kumasi-based center founded by Dr. Kyerematen was not doing anything to promote the two critical functions that he had enunciated, forgetting that Dr. Kyerematen's center never planned to have the monopoly to be either implementing or monitoring governmental policies relating to the development as well as the promotion, preservation and appreciation of culture and Ghanaian anywhere in the country, not even in the Ashanti Region, where it was based. However, supporters of Dr. Kyerematen's centre confirmed that it was already performing functions within the second segment of identifying as well as organizing and mobilizing an assortment of artistic resources of the various ethnic group regions within the context of the existing programs of the National Cultural Centre, although it was not being done for the development and commercialization potential of such resources.

To legitimize his actions, which were considered by supporters of the work of Dr. Kyerematen, including Archbishop Emeritus Sarpong, Dr. Abdallah went on to offer a definition of what he meant to be a national culture: "National culture then is a summary of selected or acceptable patterns of life from a rich shore of diverse ethnic practices within the nation, . . . national culture is a selective social process, which is achieved by integration," (Agyeman-Duah, 1995). Other memorial lecturers, similar or larger in stature, held their respective opinions.

In his very lucid foreword to *Kyerematen and Culture (The Kyerematen Memorial Lectures, 1990–1995)*, edited by Agyeman-Duah, Dr. W. Otchere Darko, as the then Director of the Centre for National Culture in Kumasi, began with an emphatic statement about Dr. Kyerematen: "Dr. Alex Atta Yaw

Kyerematen's name is associated with culture. He devoted his whole life to the promotion of Asante [or Ashanti], Ghanaian and African cultures . . . the Centre will continue through these lectures and the everlasting legacy that Dr. Alex Atta Yaw Kyerematen left to promote cultural development in Ghana" (Agyeman-Duah, 1995, p. xi).

The second distinguished lecturer, who gave his own Kyerematen Memorial Lecture on November 28, 1991, was University of Ghana's late emeritus religion professor, The Right Reverend Professor K. A. Dickson, who was at the time the president of the Conference of the Methodist Church of Ghana. His lecture was titled "Christianity and Chieftaincy: Can They Be Bed-Fellows?" Since Dr. Kyerematen, who was being honored with the memorial lecture, was a Christian as well as the formally or publicly enstooled chief of Pataase, near Kumasi, it was very appropriate that Professor Dickson's second memorial lecture took the posture of trying to find out if Christianity and chieftaincy could be bedfellows.

According to Professor Dickson, chieftaincy usually involved three crucial things, namely (a) consent of the subjects; (b) derivation of wealth in the subjects (those he ruled), and (c) the uniting of past and the present in the Chief's personality. Therefore, he elaborated in the following words: "A Chief is not supposed to be dictatorial. If he did, he would not last [in the position]" (Agyeman-Duah, 1995, p. 10). Going further to underscore the fact that, within chieftaincy, a chief often derives his wealth from his people, Professor Dickson went on to make the observation that "ideally, the Chief is supposed to be supported financially by his people. He serves his people and he is served by the subjects," (Agyeman-Duah, 1995, p. 10). At that juncture, Professor Dickson, as an eminent scholar and religious leader, explained to his audience why some of the named traits gave the church difficulty with chieftaincy, adding that the difficulty lay in the chief's role of uniting in himself the past and the present.

Among other details, he elaborated on the role of uniting the past and the present in the chief, which has been subjected to questions by the church; the queries often involve the stool as actually symbolizing the presence of the ancestors, i.e., deceased elders, who are supposed to be approached through the pouring of libation, a form of ancestral prayer. Although Professor Dickson went on to explain that a libation may not necessarily be seen as the act of worship in itself, he maintained the fact that such libation pouring could constitute an act of communing with the ancestors, which could also be an act or a petition that implies dependence, which is also an essential ingredient, adding that for a chief to sit on the stool to pour a libation does constitute "a significant religious act, which raises a serious theological issue for the church," (Agyeman-Duah, 1995, p. 11).

Also, Professor Dickson used the occasion of his memorial lecture to expatiate on the fact that, in some situations, the chief acted as a chief priest, who offers sacrifices to deities, "which are sometimes treated as ends in themselves and not just as intermediaries between God and man" (Agyeman-Duah, 1995, p. 11). Furthermore, Professor Dickson added that being a Christian also involves the following: (a) faith in Jesus Christ, implying reliance upon Christ; (b) fellowship and sacraments, thus being a Christian involving a life of sharing with others in worship; and (c) witnessing, a way of sharing one's faith with others by word and deed, (Agyeman-Duah, 1995, p. 11). Adding that, in his capacity as the head of the Methodist Church in Ghana at the time, he did not have a ready reason to doubt a chief's avowal of faith in Christ, adding that is the act of using a libation as prayer that would give an indication of a Christian commitment, adding however that giving sacrifices to deities could constitute a form of disloyalty from a Christian perspective, adding in the end: "A Chief, who expresses faith in Christ must be taken seriously, and that a Chief is not, by definition, a non-Christian," adding " a great deal depends on what the ritual requirements are and their significance," (Agyeman-Duah 1995, p. 12).

In his Kyerematen Memorial Lecture, the late Nana Professor Kwame Arhin, the former distinguished Africanist scholar as well as director of the Institute for African Studies at University of Ghana and the late professor emeritus of the university, spoke on the topic, "The Role of a Center for National Culture in National Development." Apart from lauding Dr. Kyerematen, as others have done, he also sought to discuss the Centre for National Culture as "the store-house of our past and present values, of our significant material and non-material heritage," (Agyeman-Duah, 1995, p. 13).

Very uniquely, Nana Professor Arhin—just like Dr. A. A. Y. Kyerematen—was also an enstooled chieftain in the Barekesse area, not very far from Kumasi, the Ashanti capital. In his Kyerematen Memorial Lecture, the eminent professor, who was himself educated at University of Ghana, when it was a constituent college of University of London, underscored for all and sundry in his audience to know that Dr. Kyerematen's cultural efforts were not as parochial as some critics tried to show. Instead, his collection of cultural artifacts involved pieces of artifacts found in and outside of Ghana, as he *inter alia* pointed out: Then the late President [Kwame] Nkrumah changed the name into the 'National Cultural Centre' on two possible grounds. It could well have been that Asante [or Ashanti] culture encapsulated the totality of Ghanaian culture, so that the cultural objective or activities at the [then] Asante Cultural Centre were, in fact, those of Ghana as a whole; or Nkrumah was urging Dr. Alex [Atta Yaw] Kyerematen to look beyond Asante and assemble and encourage in the Asante Cultural Centre such objects and activities as would make it representative of Ghana as a whole (Agyeman-Duah, 1995, p. 13).

Nana Professor Arhin went on, as a scholar with a vast knowledge of African geography and history, to inform his audience forcefully that Asante culture has such historic connections that it has often been a synthesis of the cultures of all the peoples, who inhabit the regions of neighboring African countries, including the Ivory Coast (or Côte d'Ivoire). He cited also that even the regalia that the Asante King or Asantehene exhibits on public occasions contains elements from the four corners of the country, adding: "The artifacts in the little museum of this Cultural Centre also tells the story, for those who know anything about the matter, of the history of Asante's connections with the peoples of Ghana and Côte d'Ivoire," (Agyeman-Duah, 1995, p. 13).

Offering his audience a lesson in cultural history, Nana Professor Arhin went on to explain that culture includes both tangible and intangible things, adding that the tangible elements of culture, in his opinion, are the means for ensuring the availability of food as well as shelter and clothing, the tools for farming, house types, and clothing, and the instruments for entertainment and the enjoyment of such leisure as afforded by drumming and dancing groups. The intangible elements of culture, as he enumerated, include the institutions for the maintenance of law and order as well as other forms of cooperation in the economic and social areas; then, he went on to add that it was also part of ensuring harmonious relations with seen and unseen power.

Toward the end of his lecture, Nana Professor Arhin discussed the different roles of the cultural center: the nurturing of proper values, usefulness of the cultural function, various regional festivals of art, the cultural centers as the store-houses of non-material values, common values and the additional role of the cultural center. In his conclusion, Nana Professor Arhin firmly urged that a cultural center, in general, "ought to be seen and act as more than recreational centers. They ought to nationalize their museums and art centers. They ought to sponsor lectures and symposia that would seek to discover the common values of our different societies, and that, therefore, would link our peoples in the search for national solidarity. Above all, to disseminate the views that come out of these lectures and symposia" (Agyeman-Duah, 1995, p. 19; Arhin, 2001).

In fact, several factors prompted us to decide to write about Dr. Kyerematen. He received both official adulation and public praise from several prominent Ghanaians as well as the common men and women of Ghana when he passed away. For example, Dr. Kyerematen was deemed so important in the context of promoting and preserving Ghana's cultural heritage that, in the early 1990s, his fellow Ghanaians instituted, in his honor, the Kyerematen Memorial Lectures. The various lectures, delivered between 1990 and 1995, have been edited, with an introduction by Ivor Agyeman-Duah, and subsequently published with the title of *Kyerematen and Culture* (Agyeman-Duah, 1999).

After considering some perplexing tribal or ethnic sentiments stemming from some non-Ashanti people, an important query to be raised is this one: Was it true that other regions had similar centres like the Kumasi-based National Cultural Centre? That was not exactly so. Instead, the suspicion was that since the PNDC commission chairman was a non-Ashanti-born Ghanaian, he either felt a sheer resentment or jealousy toward the successful creation of Dr. Kyerematen, a Ghanaian scholar who happened to be an Ashanti. In fact, in a recent interview with Catholic Archbishop Emeritus Dr. Peter Kwasi Sarpong, he expressed surprise that, instead of cherishing such a valuable center, the boss of the PNDC Commission on Culture would behave the way he did. Others who have also commented on the issue felt that since the wife of the Head of State at the time (retired Flt. Lt. J. J. Rawlings) was an Ashanti woman (i.e., Nana Agyeman Rawlings), he should have stepped in to stop what seemed like either an unnecessary interference or an under estimation of the very sacrificial cultural work of Dr. Kyerematen in Kumasi.

In fact, many Ghanaians, who have also praised Dr. Kyerematen's exemplary work on the cultural centre, have pointed out that his actions, as expressed in the publication *30 Years into Eternity*, clearly demonstrated "his awareness that Ghana's culture was a tributary of the universal cultural river of mankind," (p. 15). That was why when Ghana's then President Nkrumah, in 1962, met with Dr. Kyerematen, the reason for the Ghanaian leader deciding to assist the cultural center was that "it did not only contain replicas of the regalia of traditional rulers but, also, the specimens of the main elements of the material culture of Ghana. The ground of the center [for example] also included a model cocoa farm indicating agriculture as the main preoccupation of the farmers of this great nation of ours. Thus, any tourist visiting the place could have a feel of our rural lifestyle, which depicts most of our customs, traditions and culture" (pp. 14–15).

In spite of the obvious interference from the chairman of the PNDC's Commission on Culture, there were tributes galore from the prominent to, indeed, the very humble of Ghana's citizenry following Dr. Kyerematen's death. For example, the British-born author, Mrs. Peggy Appiah, wrote a poetic eulogy in honor of Dr. Kyerematen, titled "Dr. Alex Kyerematen, In Memoriam." She was called Lady or Aunty Peggy by the young and the old, who knew her, because of the dignified lifestyle she lived among the indigenous people of Ashanti in Kumasi, indeed, not too far from the capital. From the Kyerematen household in the Mbrom/Bantama section(s) of the Ashanti capital. She was also known as the widow of Lawyer Joseph "Joe" Appiah, a famous Ghanaian lawyer, who passed away in July of 1990. The Appiahs, like the Kyerematens, were also very famous, hence the husband's death, indeed, attracted publicity in *The New York Times*, with the headline: "Joe Appiah Is Dead; Ghanaian Politician and Ex-Envoy, 71." In the obituary, Eric Pace, *inter alia*, wrote (*The New York Times,* July 1990):

> Joe Appiah, a Ghanaian political figure and former diplomat whose marriage to a white British woman attracted wide publicity in 1953, died on Sunday in an Accra hospital, a family friend, Henry Louis Gates Jr., said. Mr. Appiah was 71 years old and lived in Kumasi, Ghana. Professor Gates, an expert in African-American literature at Duke University, said Mr. Appiah had been suffering from cancer of the mouth. (July 12, 1990)

In completing this publication, we wish to add that Dr. Kyerematen's successes in life, as partly recorded here, were due to his own staunch belief in God his Maker. That is why he and his spouse raised their children with the embodiment of a fear in God. In fact, it was not surprising that his earliest call, for which he received training, barely missed a Christian ordination following his Trinity College training, after which he left for Fourah Bay College in Sierra Leone.

It is, in fact, on such score that many Ghanaians, who became very aware of the hard work that Dr. Kyerematen put in the work of establishing the Ghana National Cultural Center, showed much admiration and respect for him. After all, he did demonstrate that nothing would disturb his life-long ambition of establishing the center. Even, before the Nkrumah Government came to his assistance with a monetary subvention each month, he did soldier on by minimizing his expenses.

DR. KYEREMATEN AS A SCHOLAR

Dr. Kyerematen, like Professor Adu-Boahen and others, produced significant books and some pamphlets on Ghana's culture. Below is a list of his works with brief descriptions of their contents:

- University of Oxford, U.K., B.Litt. Thesis: "The Determination of Traditional Boundaries in Ashanti." Doctoral (D.Phil.) dissertation: "Ashanti Royal Regalia: An Ethno-History of Ashanti Kinship." King's College, Cambridge University, U.K.
- *The Adaekese Festival* (1952)
- *Regalia for an Ashanti Durbar* (1961)
- *Panapoly of Ghana* (1964) (Intended to mark the 1964 visit of Queen Elizabeth II)
- *Kinship & Ceremony in Ashanti* (1970)

• *Ghana National Cultural Centre* (1964)

While Dr. Kyerematen's Oxford and Cambridge thesis and dissertation, respectively, fulfilled requirements for the advanced degrees he earned from both prestigious universities, his other publications were written and published with a different objective, including the fact that they underscored his true scholarly stature.

For example, his 120-page book *Panoply of Ghana* is a hardcover publication published by Longmans, Green and Company Limited, book publishers of London, UK. The 1964 book was published under the sponsorship of the Ghana Information Services, which holds the copyright. As Dr. Kyerematen has explained, *Panoply of Ghana* "was originally planned for publication in November 1959, to coincide with the visit to Ghana of Her Majesty Queen Elizabeth II, head of the Commonwealth, which was then expected to take place" (p. vii).

Most certainly, *Panoply of Ghana* was a publication that reinforced Dr. Kyerematen's cultural awareness. Since it was sponsored for publication by the Ghana Information Services Department, it benefitted tremendously from access to as well as the use of very unique photographs with cultural value. In fact, Longmans, the publishers, confirmed these details of the book, further pointing out that it was authoritative and lavishly illustrated, and that with the publication, Ghanaians should be proud of their nation's cultural heritage. According to Dr. Kyerematen, he was "commissioned in the middle of July of [1959] by the Ghana Information Services [Department] to write the script and captions for the photographs [used in the book]" (preface, p. vii).

In his own words, Dr. Kyerematen used seven chapters, a preface and an introduction to inform his readers of the unique qualities of the book for which, in his words, "there are very few publications, which have relevance to the subject-matter of this book" (preface, p. viii). Also, thematically, Dr. Kyerematen used a *Panoply of Ghana* to showcase several aspects of the country's regalia. To assist his readers to understand what regalia means, Dr. Kyerematen referred to the *Oxford English Dictionary*, which "defines regalia as the insignia of royalty used at coronations and other such occasions (introduction, p. 1). In a further explanation, Dr. Kyerematen contextualized the meaning of the regalia, which he covered extensively in his book, in the following words:

In the context of this book, however, the word [regalia] covers a much wider range of objects, from the most sacrosanct, such as the Golden Stool of the Ashanti, and the Stool of Precious Beads of the Denkyiras, to the near-ludicrous, such as an imported siphon, the aerated water from which not only quenched the chief's thirst but also delights his subjects with the hissing sound it makes (introduction, p. 1).

With an adequate understanding of the concept of regalia, Dr. Kyerematen provided information in the book based on the following sub-topics: "Stools, Skins and Chairs" (Chapter One, pp. 11–28); "Swords and Other Weapons" (Chapter Two, pp. 29–42); "The Treasury" (Chapter Three, pp. 43–56); "Musical Instruments" (Chapter Four, pp. 57–66); "Personal Ornaments" (Chapter Five, pp. 67–86); "Other Regalia" (Chapter Six, pp. 89–99); and 'Legacy of the Ghanaian Craftsman" (Chapter Seven, pp. 101–120).

HOW DR. KYEREMATEN'S OVERALL CULTURAL INFLUENCE BEARS ON AND IMPACTS THE PRESENT

When the late Emeritus Professor Nketia was paying his glowing tribute to Dr. Kyerematen's legendary pursuit of cultural awareness promotion in Ghana, he showed us a copy of the document, *The Cultural Policy of Ghana*, 2004, made up of seven chapters, with a conclusion. He agreed that the new Board of the Commission worked hard with several others to streamline Ghana's culture, which is represented in the fine document. As Dr. Nketia pointed out, the Nketia-Kyerematen cultural axis was everywhere for readers to see, but it was refashioned by younger scholars, with modern scholarly taste. From the document, we thumbed through the preamble as well as the introduction (Chapter I). There, the question was posed about Ghana's culture: What is Our Culture? Chapter II represented the objectives of the cultural policy and, indeed, its implementation, coupled with the varied approaches. Chapter III is made up of cultural education as well as a curriculum for schools and colleges. Chapter IV did constitute Ghanaian culture, as it related to the Arts.

There is what is labeled, in Chapter V, as Heritage Assets with reference to Ghana Culture, while Chapter VI relates to the Culture Industry in general. Chapters VII and VIII, respectively, deals with Mass Media as well as Culture, Science and Technology. The final part of the document ties together several aspects of Ghana Culture that has been represented in the beautiful document, which spotted, on the front cover, Ghana's Coat of Arms.

Dr. Kyerematen's earlier draft cultural document of the mid-1960s spelled out the fact that he was very much interested in showcasing the legitimacy of Ghana Culture, hence his strenuous efforts to establish, initially, the Asante Cultural Centre, which blossomed into the Ghana National Cultural Centre based in Kumasi. According to some of his publications, Dr. Kyerematen was very much tired of expatriates from Europe and the Americas giving the impression that African nations, including his beloved Ghana—earlier called the Gold Coast—had no cultural heritage of which they could boast.

In fact, that was the main reason that he agreed, with Ghana's Information Services Department, to produce *The Panoply of Ghana*, in which he single-handedly showcased cultural items from a cross-section of the country (Ghana) as part of the plans to honor the visit of Queen Elizabeth II to Ghana. From the picturesque front page to the last page of the 1964 publication, Dr. Kyerematen deliberately presented very beautiful cultural artifacts, with captions written by himself to give purpose and meaning to each covered item.

From all of Dr. Kyerematen's foregoing efforts, which culminated in the establishment of the Ghana National Cultural Centre—which received a formal boost from the government of the late President Kwame Nkrumah— one could very easily conclude that, indeed, his cultural alliance with the well-known Pan-African Nkrumah, Dr. Kyerematen was transformed into a Cultural Prince of Africa. In that capacity, he wanted to steer the continent either very clear of or away from the political chaos that several books and their authors have written to portray Africa as being in chaos; they included Economics Professor George B.N. Ayitte's *Africa in Chaos* (1998) and *Africa Betrayed* (1992).

For Dr. Kyerematen, the cultural perspectives of African nations, spearheaded by that of his beloved Ghana, were very coherent and, as a result, could be traced and codified as he did with his Ghana National Cultural Centre. Politically and economically, Africa could not be so defined. For example, Professor Ayittey quoted from *the Washington Post* newspaper of November 16, 1996 Section C1, to demonstrate a point; he alleged that the late President Mobutu of the former Zaire, now known as the Democratic Republic of the Congo (DRC), and his cronies turned "Zaire into a little more than a bankrupt kleptocracy. They bear more allegiance to their own bank balances than to their country's future" (Ayittey, 1996, p. 6). While the Ghanaian Economist—who ironically attended the same Adisadel College much later in the 1960s—could not write in a similar positive tone about either African or Ghanaian politics or economies, *per se*; he instead lamented about how Africa's endowed natural resources had been squandered; for example, he wrote: "Yet, paradoxically, a continent with such abundance and potential is inexorably mired in steaming squalor, misery, deprivation, and chaos. It is in the throes of a seemingly incurable crisis" (Ayittey, 1996, p. 7). Indeed, no writer could write about Africa's cultural heritage in similar light, thanks to Dr. A. A. Y. Kyerematen and his ardent supporters, including the traditional rulers of his Ashanti ethnic group and the national leaders of Ghana, led by the late President Kwame Nkrumah.

THE ENDURING LEGACY OF DR.
A. A. Y. KYEREMATEN

Having been born on 29th April, 1916, Dr. A. A. Y. Kyerematen was 60 years old when he died in 1976. In African age parlance, when some people live until they were in their late 80s, 90s and even a century old, the founder of the famous Ghana National Cultural Centre died relatively very young. Yet, he had done so much in his life intellectually and professionally that many of his countrymen, who honored him with a national funeral, acknowledged his greatness, thereby adding him to the heroes of the country. The heroism that was accorded Dr. Kyerematen stemmed from the fact that, for years, he had a dream that was very similar to the publicly professed dream of the late Rev. Dr. Martin Luther King, Jr. of the United States of America. Dr. King's words about his dream were pronounced in his "I Have a Dream" speech, which was publicly pronounced at the Lincoln Memorial in the American capital during his civil rights movement's march on Washington, DC on August 27, 1963.

While Dr. Kyerematen had a dream of his own, back in West Africa, the King dream was multifaceted, as it included his clarion call for his four little children, at the time, to be judged according to the contents of their characters, but not simply by the color of their black skin. Indeed, where children were concerned, the American civil rights hero's dream was not only about the four little children he had with Mrs. Coretta Scott King. Instead, he also had a dream that "one day, down in Alabama, with its vicious racists, with its governor having his lips dripping with the words of 'interposition' and 'nullification'—one day right there in Alabama little black boys and black girls will be able to join hands with little white boys and white girls as sisters and brothers." (Assensoh, 1987). It was, most certainly, a multifaceted powerful dream.

On the part of Dr. Kyerematen, he also had children, who have grown up to be wonderful adults. However, his was a dream with a singular purpose and persistence as well: just to establish a Ghana National Cultural Centre that would proudly showcase Ghana's cultural treasures to demonstrate that although Europeans, at the time, saw Africa in such primitive terms that none of its nations had a cultural heritage that was either worthy of exhibition or admiration, he was ready to prove them Europeans wrong. Therefore, he established the cultural center that today stands as part of his very much-admired legacy.

It was not only the common citizen of Ghana, in search of a center for culture to visit and pay homage to his or her eyes. Instead, Ghana's late President Kwame Nkrumah—a foremost Pan-Africanist who was voted in 2000 by listeners of the British Broadcasting Corporation (BBC) as "Africa's Man of the Millennium"—saw both the worth and also the cultural significance of the center. Therefore, he agreed to support the center financially and, in the process, to have it renamed as the Ghana National Cultural Centre. According to sources very close to the late President Nkrumah, including his own former Foreign Minister Quaison-Sackey, the America-educated leader wished that Dr. Kyerematen would become one of his closest advisers, especially with respect to matters of culture. However, the Oxford-Cambridge-educated and Kumasi-based cultural guru, eschewed partisan politics. Instead, he did not see the military-*cum*-police National Liberation Council (NLC), which succeeded the Nkrumah regime after the 1966 coup d'état, in partisan political sense.

The NLC, indeed, led Ghana's government from 24 February 1966 to 1 October 1969. It emerged from the reported CIA-instigated coup d'état against the civilian government led by President Nkrumah. The Ghana Police Service and Ghana Armed Forces jointly carried out the coup, with the visible collaboration of the leaders of the Ghana Civil Service. It is alleged that the plotters were well connected with the governments of the United Kingdom as well as the United States, who some believe approved of the coup because Nkrumah challenged their political and economic ambitions in Africa; he American leaders considered Dr. Nkrumah a closet Marxist.

Meanwhile, in his noble humane way of life, Dr. Kyerematen saw the need to extend his expertise to the military and police officers running post-Nkrumah Ghana. Therefore, when Dr. Kyerematen's fellow Adisadel College alumnus—then General Akwasi Amankwaah ("A. A.") Afrifa invited him to serve in the NLC cabinet as Secretary for local Government, he did not hesitate to serve. Since he was based in Kumasi, Dr. Kyerematen was given a government bungalow in central Accra, where he lived with his family in order to serve as Secretary for Local Government. In his cabinet-level position as Secretary for Local Government, an enviable central policy Dr. Kyerematen tried to cultivate was to assist the National Liberation Council to have a coherent cultural policy, with himself playing a central role. Although he was very careful not to import his Kumasi-based Ghana National Cultural Centre to the Local Government Ministry, it was not impossible that he tried to educate the police and military usurpers of Ghana politics at the time.

It is, therefore, to Dr. Kyerematen's credit that post-Nkrumah Ghana saw regimes, both coup-installed and elected, espousing strong cultural sentiments and even written policies. Therefore, even in death, Dr. Kyerematen's strongest legacy is to be remembered as the cultural prince of both Ghana and Africa.

BUILDING ON DR. KYEREMATEN'S LASTING LEGACY

Among notable citizens of Ghana, who have paid unlimited tributes to Dr. Kyerematen's cultural awareness message over the years was University of Ghana's late Emeritus Professor J.H. Kwabena Nketia, who passed away in Ghana on Wednesday, March 13, 2019, aged 97 years. As expected, we are among the teeming number of men and women, who have visited a legacy website to pay glowing tributes to his memory. In fact, it is not surprising that where Ghana's cultural interests are concerned, the late Emeritus Professor Nketia and Dr. Kyerematen did stand very tall. However, in our interview with him, the distinguished ethnomusicologist (Dr. Nketia) promptly deferred to Dr. Kyerematen. It was, however, interesting that the National Commission on Culture acknowledged, with appreciation, the pioneering effort of Emeritus Professor Nkekia, as it is confirmed in an acknowledgment, in fashioning out a Cultural Policy document for Ghana soon after it attained nationhood in 1957.

This maiden policy was adopted by UNESCO and since then successive governments have used it as a reference point," (Ghana National Commission on Culture, 2001: Acknowledgment page). Historically, the Commission went on to add that, in 1983, the first elaborate work on such a policy was made under the political headship of Mr. Asiedu Yirenkyi, the then Secretary for Culture and Tourism in the erstwhile Provisional National Defence Council (PNDC). His successor Dr. Mohammed Ben Abdallah, ably assisted by Dr. (Mrs.) Esi Sutherland-Addy and Mr. Walter Blege, reviewed the document when the National Commission on Culture was established by PNDC Law 238 in 1990. Prof Kwame Arhin and his successor, Nana Akuaku Sarpong, undertook a series of revisions and had the Draft Policy discussed at cabinet level but it did not receive assent then. In the year 2001, under the Presidency of His Excellency J. A. Kufuor, George P. Hagan, Chairman, and the Commissioners identified the absence of a policy as a major hindrance to the entire document culminating in a Stakeholders Workshop in Kumasi. Today, we are happy to note that the efforts of the pioneers have not been in vain. "We Build on the Old," says an adage. "The goal of fashioning a Cultural Policy for Ghana has been achieved" (Ibid., 2001).

Also, the National Commission, which was chaired by the Honorable George P. Hagan, did in writing acknowledge the invaluable contributions of all statesmen, policy makers, politicians, chiefs and people of Ghana, whose combined efforts engineered the published policy. Impressively, the commission added that, with culture being dynamic, "it is an undeniable fact that the document will, from time to time, be reviewed to reflect the changing needs of time," (*Ibid.*, 2001). Furthermore, special thanks and appreciation were registered for the Konrad Adenauer Foundation and the Goethe Institute of Germany for sponsoring an International workshop, which brought Stakeholders to Kumasi to share their views on the formulated policy.

In our interview with the late University of Ghana Emeritus Professor Kwame Arhin—himself an enstooled royal chieftain of Ghana's Barekesse area, similar to the royal status of Dr. Kyerematen at Patase—he acknowledged unlimitedly that among the distinguished Ghanaians the Commission had in mind to thank and appreciate was Dr. Kyerematen, adding that he (Dr. Arhin) thought that it was an oversight that he was not mentioned in name in the document. In our interview, Dr. Arhin, who died on September 6, 2015, added humorously: "A. B., you are a bona fide historian, and your co-author from America, too, is a political scientist and a lawyer of repute. So, you can very easily remember dots and knots when discussing an issue. In fact, I am even happy that the post-independent yeoman's work of Emeritus Professor Nketia, which was with a documentary evidence, was acknowledged the way it was done in the published *Ghana Cultural Policy* in 2001."

Meanwhile, many admirers of Dr. Kyerematen have been satisfied by the clarion calls for him to be publicly recognized for his work in establishing the Ghana National Cultural Centre. It was in such circumstance that a major Ghanaian traditional leader and the center's former director Nana Brefo Boateng, who publicly urged his fellow Ghanaians to name the Cultural Centre after Dr Kyerematen, the founder and the first director of the center. His clarion call was made during the Kwame Nkrumah Centenary Lectures, which were organized by the Cultural Initiatives Support Program, (CISP), which was under the auspices of the National Commission on Culture; the series was funded by the European Development Fund (EDF), and its public function took place on Wednesday, September, 30, 2009 at the Centre for National Culture in Kumasi; the impressively large function was chaired by Oheneba Adusei Poku, the local *Akyempemhene* (a local chieftain title).

Nana Boaten, *inter alia*, added: "It is with much pleasure therefore as the then Programs Officer for the Cultural Initiatives Support Programme and a Deputy Director (on Leave) of Centre for National Culture, Kumasi, and now a Lecturer at the University of Ghana, Legon to recount how Dr. Alexander Atta Yaw Kyerematen selflessly sowed the cultural seed for us so that all and sundry will know and appreciate his efforts."

To Nana Boateng, a sociologist by training and at the time teaching at University of Ghana, added that the Cultural Centre was built on the sacrifices of certain individuals, led by Dr. Kyerematen. "Most of the works carried out at the Centre, particularly during the early parts of its establishment, was accomplished through local voluntary donations and communal labor. Thus, a careful look at the Centre's achievements should not fail to give a convincing proof to everyone that, the result has been more than justified, the dreams and aspirations of the Centre's Founding Fathers, again led by Dr. Alexander Atta Yaw Kyerematen. His name is noted to be the brain behind the famous Cultural Centre in Kumasi. It is to him and his family so much does the Centre owe its very birth and growth. He became the Founder and the First Director of the Centre," he added to a very thunderous applause.

Quoting from the late Ama Ata Aidoo, one of the veteran female writers in Ghana, Nana Boaten went on to tell his audience that, as Aidoo wrote in his published play, "The Dilemma of a Ghost," the day of planning is always different from the day of battle. Help for the establishment of the center, as he disclosed further at the function, came from Asanteman Council of Chiefs; he explained that after so many attempts to get financial support to begin the work of the center, Dr. Kyerematen took a bold step and approached the Asanteman Council of Chiefs "to convince (or lobby) Nananom of the immense benefits which the people of Asante could derive from the proposed cultural center. God being so good all the time, he had the audience with Nananom and for the first time since he started his campaign to establish the center, some amount of money was raised in donations through the selfless nature and gesture by which members of the Asanteman Council of Chiefs showed. To prove their interest in the project, they decided to forego their sitting allowances for that day towards the project. It was like a dream to see the old Asante spirit of oneness in times of difficulties and national crisis, spring to life so suddenly and so assuredly as heavy rains. The battle was half won and that night, the haggard-looking and weary Kyerematen had a long peaceful sleep, which took the wife Mrs. Victoria Kyerematen a long time to wake him up," Nana Boateng disclosed to an applause as well. In the end, he called on his fellow Ghanaians to rename the center in honor of Dr. Kyerematen, something that Emeritus Catholic Archbishop Peter Akwasi Sarpong felt that he would not have liked it, indeed due to his modesty in life (see profile of the Emeritus Archbishop in the appendices section of the book).

Chapter 6

The Lasting Legacy

The Kyerematen Family of Ghana

Apart from his rich cultural heritage and the bequeathing of the centre to Ghana, he also left an enduring family heritage. For example, when he passed away in 1976, his nuclear family members—who survived him—included his widow, Lady (Mrs.) Victoria Kyerematen (*née* Wesling) as well as their very successful children: Mr. Stephen ("Steve") Osei Tutu Kyerematen, retired managing director of Activa International Insurance Company (Ghana) Limited; former Ghana Trade Minister Alan John Kwadwo Kyerematen (a trained lawyer and economist and, like his late father, an Adisadel College alumnus). Dr. Kyerematen was also survived by Dr. Gabriel Augustine Kwasi Dwira Kyerematen, a very prominent physician in Raleigh, North Carolina, USA; Rev. Richard Kyerematen, a prominent pastor of a famous church in Germantown, Pennsylvania, USA; the late Mrs. Bridget Margaret Akosua Asogyaa Kyerematen-Darko, executive director of Aid to Artisans Ghana (ATAG); and Madlene Serwaa Kobi Kyerematen (Maame Serwaa), who earned her master of fine arts (MFA) postgraduate degree from the Washington, DC-based Howard University in the United States.

When we interviewed his widow (admirably referred to as Lady Victoria Kyerematen), she pointed out, among other laudable details, that Dr Kyerematen was known to have spent his last dollar on the centre to ensure its success. Therefore, he could not afford to buy a house of his own for his family. Instead, it was a European couple, who initially assisted the family to get a place in which they lived until much later on that they owned a house of their own. As a real life partner of Dr. Kyerematen, Lady Victoria sacrificed to take care of the young family, especially when Dr. Kyerematen was away in England pursuing his doctoral degree. Despite the heavy load that she carried, she not only survived but thrived, working with Dr. Kyerematen to produce children who are model citizens in Ghana, America and beyond. Mrs. Kyerematen—affectionately dubbed as Lady Victoria, whose own royal background hails from Ejisu, near Kumasi, and Elmina in the Central Region—was 94 years old in 2014 (*Africawatch*, May 2014:18); she celebrated her 101st birthday in 2021. When Dr. Alexander Atta Yaw (A.A.Y.). Kyerematen passed away in 1976, Mrs. Victoria Joanna Kyerematen (*nee* Welsing) effectively became the matriarch of the Kyerematen Family of Kumasi and Patase, near the Ashanti capital, where the West African cultural prince (Dr. Kyerematen) exercised functions of royalty in his lifetime.

As a family man, Dr. Kyerematen, who was known to be very busy with the leadership and running of his Kumasi-based National Cultural Center had a nephew from Patase, Mr. Akwasi Pipim (Uncle Teng to the four sons and two daughters), who assisted in dealing with the young children on daily basis. In an interview with 83-year-old nephew Pipim at his Maryland home, he confirmed what the youngsters had said to us about his involvement in their daily welfare, which included taking them to and picking them from school.

With the uncle (Dr. Kyerematen) being an Anthropologist, it was not surprising that Mr. Pipim also chose to earn an Anthropology degree from Fordham University in New York. Upon completion, he took a job with the Smithsonian Institute, which included helping with the running of the African-American Cultural Museum of the Smithsonian Institute. He takes pride in the fact that he helped in raising the six Kyerematen children and that, in reciprocity, they have a lot of admiration or affection for one another. Today, he is a father of six children of his own.

STEPHEN (STEVE) KYEREMATEN: A MAJOR FORCE IN THE INTERNATIONAL INSURANCE INDUSTRY

The oldest of the six Kyerematen siblings is Mr. Stephen (Steve) Kyerematen (or Nana Osei), the well-known international insurance guru. In fact, when donating 1,500 bags of cement for the construction of the Christian Worship Center of the Kumasi-based Kwame Nkrumah University of Science and Technology (KNUST) in July of 2021, Ghana's former Trade and Industry Minister Alan Kwadwo Kyerematen, the third-born sibling, pointed out the fact that he had, *per se*, not attended KNUST; instead, *Home General News* reporter Philip Quateh quoted him as informing the audience: "Three of my siblings are alumni of the university [KNUST]. My late father, Dr. Alexander Atta Yaw Kyerematen was Chairman of the University Council, many years back." (Quateh, July 10, 2021: p. 2). In fact, Mr. Steve Kyerematen was one of the three siblings, who attended KNUST.

With his KNUST education, Mr. Steve Kyerematen branched into the international insurance sector, and he has distinguished himself. Therefore, between 2009 and 2017, he served successfully as the Managing Director and

Chief Executive Officer (CEO) of ACTIVA International Insurance Company Limited. On July 26, 2017, the board, staff, and stakeholders of the company hosted an auspicious retirement event in his honor at the Accra-based Movenpick Ambassador Hotel.

Indeed, as announced at the event, Mr. Steve Kyerematen was retiring from what was described as very heavy responsibilities. They included having consecutively been serving as the Vice-Chairman of ACTIVA Ghana, Chairman of ACTIVA Liberia, Chairman of ACTIVA Sierra Leone, and Managing Director of ACTIVA Financial Limited, positions in which he was being replaced that year by his fellow Ghana-born Mr. Solomon Lartey.

At his retirement event, one could infer the importance of Mr. Steve Kyerematen by the important personalities, who attended; apart from his brother as a cabinet member of the Ghana Government, also attending were Ghana's Insurance Commissioner Lydia Lariba Bawa, Groupe ACTIVA Board members as well as Group Chairman and President Richard Lowe; Ghana Insurance Association President Aretha Duku; Ghana Insurance Brokers' Association President Natan Adu; Ghana Insurance Institute's President Rev. Ahenkora Marfo as well as several Managing Directors, Chief Executive Officers, Executive Directors of Ghana and many other leaders of the local insurance industry.

As clearly spelled out at the major July 2017 event honoring retiring Steve Kyerematen, ACTIVA was created in Cameroon in 1998 with a "vision and ambition to build an African champion capable of delivering fit insurance solutions to individuals and corporations throughout the continent. Almost 20 years later, we have active subsidiaries in 5 countries (hopefully 7 countries by the of the year, 2017), and a network, GLOBUS, which covers 47 countries" (ACTIVA news release, 2017: p.1). He (Nana Osei) and his wife, Mrs. Adwoa Kyerematen, have three children, Jane, Alex, and Charles.

GABRIEL A. KYEREMATEN, MD. (AGYA): A DISTINGUISHED PRACTITIONER OF MEDICINE

With more than 25 years of medical practice in the area of Internal Medicine, with a specialization in Adolescence Medicine, Dr. Gabriel A. Kyerematen ("Agya") is a well-known Physician in the Raleigh, North Carolina, area with his nuclear family: Mrs. Roseth Kyerematen and twin daughters, Victoria (Mama Vic) and Alexandra (Maame Serwaa). The daughters are trained in Medicine and Law, respectively. Available public information on Dr. Gabriel A. Kyerematen's medical practice rates him as a much sought-after Medical Practitioner.

Dr. Gabriel Kyerematen, who earned his medical degree from the Medical College of Pennsylvania, is one of three Kyerematen siblings, who studied at the Kwame Nkrumah University of Science and Technology (KNUST) in Kumasi, Ghana. Popularly known as Agya, the future Dr. Gabriel Kyerematen proceeded to the United States with plans to seek either higher education or a professional degree. Therefore, it did not surprise other Kyerematen family members when—as the second oldest Kyerematen sibling—he successfully studied for the Medical College Admission Test (MCAT) and, upon doing very well, he entered the Medical College of Pennsylvania in Philadelphia, also known as MCP-Hahnemann College of Medicine, which had been named in honor of Samuel Hahnemann, the homeopathic medicine founder. However, when young Gabriel attended, it was simply known as The Medical College of Pennsylvania.

ALAN JOHN KWADWO KYEREMATEN: POLITICIAN, DIPLOMAT & AN INTERNATIONAL PUBLIC SERVANT

Born in the Ashanti regional capital of Kumasi on October 3, 1955, Alan—as he is simply known, but sometimes nicknamed "Alan Cash"—was named in honor of a British Church of England (or Anglican) Archbishop. In his elaborate interview with *Africawatch Magazine*, in which he underscored Ghana's need for a transformational leadership, Lawyer Alan Kyerematen confirmed the foregoing facts in the following words:

As [it] is often the case in Christian families in Ghana, I was given an "*oburoni*'" (English) name and a 'traditional' name. I was named after an Anglican archbishop from England, the Most Rev. Alan John Knight, who was the first headmaster of Adisadel College in Cape Coast. He was a mentor to my father when he was a student and the first head prefect of the same school in the 1930s. I was also named after my parental grand-uncle, Chief Atta Akwasi, Abenasehene (chief of the royal wardrove of the late Asantehene, Otumfuo [Sir] Osei Agyeman Prempeh II, one of the most celebrated Asante kings. This is the genesis of my name "Chief" by which I am affectionately called by family and close associates. (*Africawatch Magazine, ibid.*: p.18)

Very remarkably, as young Alan had earlier pointed out, he subsequently added that since he carried himself well for people in their neighborhood to think that he and his older two siblings were triplets in terms of weight or size, his parents were inclined to send him to start elementary (or primary) school at the age of four, instead of the traditional age of either 6 or above at the time. Young Alan, therefore, confirmed how he entered Adisadel College at an unprecedentedly young age but succeeded:

> It was against this background that my parents were forced to take me to primary school at an early age of four years, when the average start age was six years and above in those days. Fortunately, I did not only survive but competed well enough, in spite of my age, to have been able to gain admission to Adisadel College at a record age of nine years. Thereafter, I attended the famous Achimota School for my sixth form education, where I was nominated and elected as the chief of the Twi ethnic group, as part of our extracurricular cultural program. (*Africawatch Magazine, ibid.*:p. 18)

With his acquisition of the relevant entrance qualifications, young Alan entered University of Ghana at Legon and, as he pointed out as well, he added: "I proceeded to the University of Ghana, Legon, and graduated with a bachelors honors degree in economics in 1976. Subsequently, I took another course in law from 1980 to 1984 and qualified as a barrister at law from the Ghana Law School" (*Africawatch, ibid*: p. 18).

Since qualifying as a Lawyer (or Barrister at Law), Alan Kyerematen has distinguished himself in a variety of ways, including serving for several years as a principal consultant and head of Public Systems Management with a Ghana-based Management Development and Productivity Institute and, also, as a public servant for the UN's Economic Commission for Africa (UN-ECA) in Addis Ababa, Ethiopia; a former Ambassador for Ghana in the USA as well as serving, as of 2003, in the second term of the Kufuor Administration as Trade and Industry Minister and, formerly, in the two terms of the Akufo-Addo Administration. Before that, he competed very well as a presidential candidate at the national party level of the NPP. Internationally, Alan Kyerematen was Ghana-nominated unsuccessful director-general candidate of the World Trade Organization (WTO), with the strong support of the African Union (AU).

Apart from serving the United Nations' Development Program (UNDP) in Africa at an executive level, he as well negotiated a $45 million facility with the World Bank for the promotion of the development of small and medium enterprise in Ghana. Back in Ghana, Alan Kyerematen served Ghana's ruling political party (NPP) at national executive level from 1992 to 2001.

Alan Kyerematen, who prides himself as a family man, is married to Mrs. Patricia Christabel Kyerematen (*nee* Kingsley-Nyinah). They are the parents of two children, Alexander and Victor Kyerematen. In his usual entrepreneurial spirit, Alan Kyerematen and his older brother (Insurance guru Stephen Kyerematen) have established and are serving as Managing Directors of A Wealth of Women (Ghana BKD) Foundation, which is in honor of the legacy of their sister (Mrs. Bridget Kyerematen-Darko), who died tragically in the gas explosion accident in Accra, Ghana in 2017.

MRS. BRIDGET KYEREMATEN-DARKO (1957–2017)

Mrs. Bridget Kyerematen-Darko was one of the six Kyerematen siblings; she tragically died from injuries she sustained from the La Gas station explosion, near the Ghanaian capital, Accra. She was the Executive Director of Aid to Artisans, Ghana (ATAG), a non-governmental organization (NGO) that was established in 1989 to support the development of the Craft Industry in Ghana. After her initial education from the famous Achimota College, she studied Development Planning for her first degree, and also earned a post-graduate diploma in Industrial Management, both from the Kwame Nkrumah University of Science and Technology (KNUST). She subsequently received an MBA (in Finance) from University of Ghana and subsequently completed the prestigious Program on Investment Appraisal and Management at the Harvard Institute for International Development. She since then participated in several other training programs, apart from her extensive work experience in both the public and private.

Nationally, Mrs. Kyerematen-Darko worked in the Cocoa Sector as a Projects Officer, and later joined the Ghana Ministry of Finance and worked with a team on its Private Sector Reform program. She left the Ministry to join Aid to Artisans, Ghana (ATAG) in 1993, and remained with the organization until her untimely death in 2017. In her ATAG leadership capacity, she assisted with the development of new products for the craft industry and search for new raw materials to sustain production throughout Ghana. She also worked on the expansion of the external market for craft products, the infusion of new technology, including ICT into the industry, provision of credit facility for producers, industry collaboration with tertiary education.

The late Mrs. Kyerematen-Darko was well traveled and, a result, gained considerable experiences from her travels to the USA, Canada, Holland, England, Israel, India, Honduras, Ecuador as well as throughout Africa, where she visited Morocco, Burkina Faso, Nigeria, Cameroon, Tanzania, Kenya, Benin, Ivory Coast, South Africa, and Senegal, among others. She was married to the late Mr. Emmanuel Darko of Accra, Ghana, with whom they had two brilliant children, young Emmanuel ("Manny"), a graduate of Northwestern University; and Margaret, also a graduate of Duke University in North Carolina and currently a medical student in the USA.

REVEREND RICHARD KYEREMATEN, PASTOR OF CHURCH OF THE BRETHREN, GERMANTOWN, PENNSYLVANIA, USA

Reverend Richard Kyerematen, born in Ghana on November 28, 1959, is the fifth child of Dr. A.A.Y. Kyerematen. He came to America to complete his seminary studies, and he has, since 1989, been the Pastor of Germantown (Pennsylvania) Church of the Brethren. As a mother church to the U.S. Protestant denomination, the church celebrated its 300th year of existence in 2019. The long history dates back to when Germantown was a suburb of Philadelphia, and that the church traces its religious ancestry to the early 18th century Brethren movement in Schwartzenau, Germany.

Rev. Kyerematen, who prefers that his church's history should dominate his personal life achievements, narrated the fact that 1719 has been recorded in *Church of the Brethren Yearbook* as the date that his church's congregation started although, to the best of his knowledge, the formal formation of the congregation was not until 1723, while the first part of the historic building was constructed in 1776. Pastor Kyerematen recalled that several additions were made in 1894 and 1914 to the building. However, 1723 was when the first Brethren baptisms the Americas took place on Christmas day in the Wissahickon River in Pennsylvania. Pastor Kyerematen explains how love is a major tenet of the Christian faith of their Church of the Brethren, which was founded by Germans, who migrated to America in search of a place, where they could very freely practice their religious beliefs.

Dr. Kyerematen's youngest son pointed the following out about his 1989 arrival at the church, after his seminary training: "When I was called in, this was the second attempt to rebuild the congregation. It was just the challenges that all churches faced in the '60's and the congregation had a whole time coming out of it but I'm glad that the denomination didn't give up and that we are now blessed with a solid congregation." He added how the congregation of the church consists of an eclectic community of diverse groups of people from different backgrounds and cultures worshipping together. Church member Derek Carter, who has been worshipping there for over four years, in an interview pointed out: "It's a special church." He added that the congregation has "a gambit of people from all denominations."

MADELENE KYEREMATEN (MAAME SERWAA)

Popularly known as Maame Serwaa, Ms. Madelene Kyerematen is a graduate of the Kwame Nkrumah University of Science and Technology (KNUST), from where two of her other older siblings also studied and graduated. Their father, Dr. Alexander Atta Yaw (A.A.Y.) Kyerematen teamed up with Roman Catholic's Emeritus Archbishop Peter Akwasi Sarpong to serve KNUST very well as active members of its Governing Council. Indeed, both the distinguished cultural prince and the well-known Emeritus Catholic Prelate—the two graduates of the famous University of Oxford in Anthropology, respectively—served as Chairmen of the KNUST Council.

Upon migrating from Ghana to the U.S.A. Madelene Kyerematen entered Howard University, popularly known as the Black Mecca, to study in a graduate program in Fine Art; after earning her Master of Fine Arts (MFA) degree, she worked for various American institution before she decided to return home, to make sure that someone was around to assist her long-surviving mother and widow of the African cultural prince (Dr. Kyerematen).

In addition to Ms. Madelene Kyerematen representing the Kyerematen siblings in assisting their mother (Lady Victoria), she is a private entrepreneur in Kumasi, the Ashanti regional capital, where she takes care of her mother and does private entrepreneur work, including her import-*cum*-export business.

Currently, all the Kyerematen hands are on deck to promote the A Wealth of Women (Ghana BKD) Foundation, which is in honor of the legacy of their sister (Mrs. Bridget Kyerematen-Darko), who died tragically in 2017 in the La gas explosion accident near Accra. It was, indeed, an occasion that brought former and sitting Ghanaian presidents, who attended her final funeral rites at the Anglican Church's cathedral in Kumasi, Ghana. As researchers and co-authors for the volume on her late father, we attended the funeral rites in Ghana, during which Yvette spoke on our behalf.

Most certainly, from their collective achievements, the Kyerematen siblings have lived and performed so creditably that their late father, Dr. Alexander Atta Yaw Kyerematen, will rest in perfect peace, while the entire family re-echo the Caesarian words, with minor modification: "We came, we saw, we conquered!"

In addition to the living legacy that Dr. Kyerematen left to Ghana through his children, he and his wife Lady Victoria also worked hard to leave a legacy in the built environment.

DR. KYEREMATEN'S LEGACY: CULTURE
IN THE BUILT ENVIRONMENT

Dr. Kyerematen was very well-known for the Ghana National Cultural Centre that he established and, over the years, promoted it to make it become a national treasure. However, as his archival records have also shown, he was, as well, a very busy and successful businessman. In 1974, barely two years before he passed away, he and his wife, Lady Victoria, teamed up to establish the Vicalex Brick and Tile Company (VBT).

To be known as "The Village," Dr. Kyerematen and Mrs. Victoria Kyerematen (who chose to go by her unmarried name, Victoria Ama Amissah) spelled out the original vision of the business company to include making it a tourist attraction, where there was to be a demonstration of the production of local crafts; the foremost craft was the production of pottery products as well as small quantities of hand-made bricks. There was a need for the diversification of products to be produced by the Vicalex Brick and Tile Company. As an active member of the governing council of the Kwame Nkrumah University of Science and Technology (KNUST), of which he was also the elected chairman, the VBT company sought the assistance of KNUST's Building and Road Research Institute (B.R.R.I.) in order to concentrate on the production of only bricks and tiles, as well as ensuring that the local company would become fully automated. Subsequently, the company was transformed into a modern multi-million-dollar brick and tile company. From the records of the Kyerematen company, VBT has become the brick and tile industry's leader in the production and supply of the products to very dedicated customers of what was known as an emerging and growing residential, commercial and industrial housing company, which exclusively uses clay products that can be found in every part of Ghana and outside. In terms of peak production, VBT had the capacity to produce 40,000 bricks daily. In a mission statement, they wrote, *inter alia*, that it was dedicated to the production of "high-quality diversified brick and products to meet all the building needs" of its customers. It added: "Ultimately, our goal is to be a major contributor to the development of a modern housing industry nation-wide emphasizing the use of locally manufactured building products" (http://www .vicalexbrickghana.com/aboutUs.html).

Even after Dr. Kyerematen's death, the very successful company survived him, as its manager happened to be Mr. John Asare, one of the industry's leading experts, who served for a while as the national chairman of the Brick and Tile Manufacturing Association of Ghana. For continuing smooth-running of the company, a seven-member board was appointed to oversee the business affairs of the company. A subsidiary of the company is Allied Construction and Environmental Services, while its affiliate companies include the Ghana Affordable Housing Project as well as the Ghana Rural Housing Project.

In fact, the available records have indicated that the Vicalex Brick and Title Company—which uses a mixture of the first two names of the founders, Victoria and Alex—contributes immensely to the employment of many Ghanaian citizens. Also, it has promoted affordable housing, whereby

Ghanaians living abroad are able to send funds to acquire parcels of land and, in the end, to use family members to start building for them brand new housing units, most of which are not as expensive as other companies charge.

With the capacity to transform places, including towns and hamlets, with what VBT describes as durable, low-cost, sustainable, modern housing units, the names of the founders—the Kyerematens—have become household names, thus adding to the enduring legacy of Dr. A. A. Y. Kyerematen, Africa and Ghana's cultural prince.

Appendix A

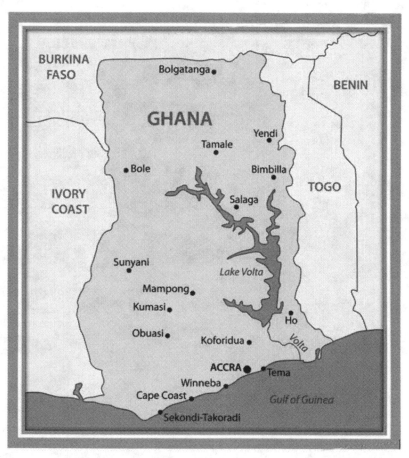

Appendix A.1. Author's modification of Department of Peacekeeping Operations Cartographic Section: A Detailed cultural map of Ghana after 1957. Courtesy of the authors. Created by Dr. Augustine Adu Frimpong.

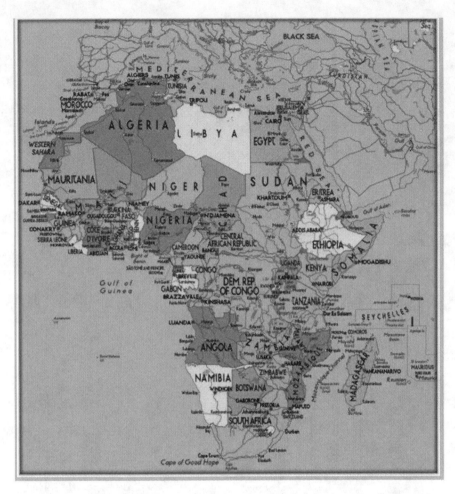

Appendix A.2. A cultural map of Africa after Ghana became a Republic on July 1, 1960. Courtesy of the authors. Created by Dr. Augustine Adu Frimpong.

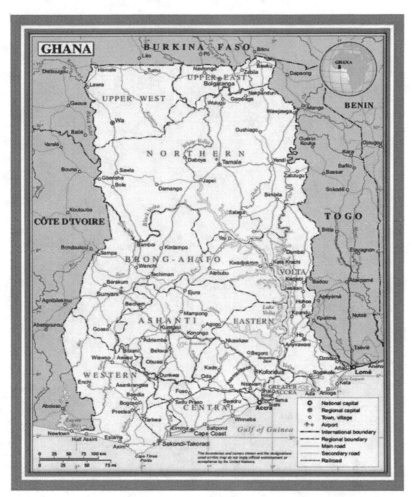

Appendix A.3. This is seen as a cultural map of Dr. Kyerematen's Ghana. Discussed at our endowed cultural lecture. Courtesy of the authors. Created by Dr. Augustine Adu Frimpong.

Appendix B

A Brief Profile Of Interviewed Catholic Archbishop Emeritus Dr. Peter Kwasi Sarpong, A Close Contemporary Of Dr. A. A. Y. Kyerematen, Both Of Whom Studied Anthropology At Oxford. He Was Interviewed In May Of 2017 For The Book..

WHO IS CATHOLIC ARCHBISHOP EMERITUS SARPONG?

Based in Kumasi, Ashanti Region's capital of Ghana, Archbishop Emeritus Most Rev. Dr. Peter Kwasi Sarpong happened to be a very close friend and professional colleague of the late Dr. A. A. Y. Kyerematen. Both of them were graduates of University of Oxford, where they studied Anthropology at different levels. An interview with him has been integrated into the text of the book. However, this very short profile is for readers to know his exceptional background, which is very much similar in quality to that of Dr. Kyerematen. As his Assistants agreed with us, in our face-to-face interview, it has certainly been a long journey for the Catholic prelate emeritus, who described himself as a very dear friend of Dr. Kyerematen as well as his Kumasi-based nuclear family. Catholic Archbishop Emeritus Sarpong, has risen from humble beginnings to the top of the Kumasi Diocese of the Roman Catholic Church.

Even, in birth, Dr. Kyerematen and the Catholic prelate emeritus had similar circumstances, including the fact that both of them hailed from the Ashanti ethnic group, and they had Christian upbringings: Sarpong as a Roman Catholic, and Kyerematen as a member of the Church of England (or Anglican Church). Sarpong was born on Sunday, February 26, 1933 at Offinso-Maase in the Ashanti Region of Ghana, and he was formally named as Kwasi Sarpong Kumankuma (a last name that, in the indigenous Asante Language meant "the killer of heroes"). Also, just like the young Kyerematen, he was educated in local elementary schools and later pursued his seminary training at the Catholic seminary at Amisano, Central Region of Ghana, where he would later in life play a leadership role.

Very interestingly, as a youngster Dr. Kyerematen too attended an Accra-based Protestant divinity school before he chose to travel to Sierra Leone to attend Fourah Bay College. The young Sarpong went on to travel to Rome to study at a Catholic university, where he earned his undergraduate and a postgraduate (master's) degree. Upon his return to Ghana, then Rev. Sarpong served in various capacities until he became the third Bishop of the Catholic Church in Ghana, but he was the second indigenous Bishop of the Kumasi Diocese. At the time, the Kumasi and Brong Ahafo Diocese was very much separated from the Gold Coast Vicariate. Before then Bishop Sarpong and other Bishops, who had served the Diocese of Kumasi and, as he pointed out in our interview with him in May of 2017, generously paved the way for his ascension in the Catholic Church of Ghana, which at the time had a prominent church leader in the Cape Coast-based Archbishop.

Archbishop Emeritus Sarpong explained that he regarded Catholic Archbishop John Kodwo Amissah (November 27, 1922–September 22, 1991) as a great mentor. The older Ghanaian prelate of the Catholic Church served as Archbishop of Cape Coast from 1959 until his death in 1991. Born in Elmina, he was ordained to the Catholic priesthood on December 11, 1949. Similar to Dr. Kyerematen and then Bishop Sarpong, he studied abroad, as he entered St. Peter's College in Rome to study for his degrees, where his honors degree thesis was on a comparison between canon law and Ghana's native customs of marriage. Being older than Sarpong, he was ordained a Catholic priest on December 11, 1959, two years after Ghana became an independent nation. In 1964, he earned his master of theology degree from the University of St. Thomas Aquinas in Rome. Just like Kyerematen and Sarpong later, the young and ambitious Amissah also studied at Oxford, from where he earned his Doctor of Philosophy (D.Phil.) degree in Social Anthropology. Based in the Central Region of Ghana, Amissah became the resident Bishop of the Catholic Diocese and, in his rapid promotion to become an Archbishop, he became an itinerant prelate as he travelled throughout the Eastern and Western Regions of Ghana to perform confirmation activities for baptized Catholic communicants.

It is, therefore, not gainsaying when Sarpong regarded the late Archbishop Amissah as a mentor. He, therefore, returned to Ghana after his overseas studies to serve the local (Ashanti) Catholic Church as well as Ghana in a variety of positions. For example, he served as the official Chaplain of the Okomfo Anokye Teaching Hospital in Kumasi and also as the Assistant Parish Priest at St. Peter's Cathedral in the city. At the time, Dr. Kyerematen was on the board Directors of the hospital, and it was confirmed by the Catholic prelate that it was the time that their friendship blossomed. Very much unlike the situation of Dr. Kyerematen, who preferred to be based in Kumasi in order to nurture his cultural centre ambitions, the young Catholic priest was instead transferred from the city, as he was appointed the Rector of St. Peter's Major Seminary in the Central Region of Ghana, and it was deemed an honor, as it was the first time that an African prelate held the position at any major Catholic seminary in Ghana. When serving at St. Peter's Major Seminary, Rev. Sarpong's appointment, as a bishop, was announced. At the seminary, he performed a dual responsibility as an Administrator and a Lecturer. Instead, he was subsequently appointed the young Bishop of Kumasi in 1969 (at the age of 37 years), but it was in 1970 that he was consecrated at St. Peter's Cathedral in Kumasi. Therefore, he took possession of the Cathedral as well as the Diocese of Kumasi and Brong Ahafo, now known as the Metropolitan Archdiocese of Kumasi of the Roman Catholic Church in Ghana. Very interestingly, the young Bishop Sarpong was actively operating in Kumasi and Brong Ahafo areas at the same time that Dr. Kyerematen was in Kumasi working hard to establish his centre, which later became a tremendous national asset that attracted the attention of the national leader, then President Kwame Nkrumah.

DR. KYEREMATEN SERVES KNUST WITH ARCHBISHOP SARPONG

Established in 1952, the Kwame Nkrumah University of Science and Technology (KNUST) was formerly known as the University of Science and Technology (UST). The name of Ghana's late President Kwame Nkrumah was attached to it to honor what the first indigenous President of Ghana did to promote the institution to make it a viable educational institution of higher learning, thus becoming KNUST. Then Bishop Sarpong and Dr. Kyerematen were long-term members of the University's Council, the governing body. In our interview with him Archbishop Emeritus Sarpong pointed out unequivocally that he was very happy to serve the Council with Dr. Kyerematen as its Chairman. Therefore, Dr. Kyerematen's dear friend, Archbishop Sarpong, a fellow Ashanti ethnic group member, served in the high Catholic Church position of Archbishop from 17th January 2002 to 26th of March 2008.

As Bishop, since 1969, he and Dr. Kyerematen served on several local boards, but he pointed out to us in the interview that the most memorable was the University Council of Kwame Nkrumah University of Science and Technology (KNUST). The institution's governance is carried out by the high-powered Council, primarily, through the Academic Board, which is responsible for:

- formulating and carrying out the academic policy of the university

- devising and regulating the courses of instruction and study, and supervising research
- regulating the conduct of examinations and the award of degrees, diplomas and certificates
- advising the University Council on the admission of students and the award of scholarships
- reporting on such matters as may be referred to it by the University Council

It is, therefore, not surprising that upon Dr. Kyerematen's death, then Catholic Bishop Sarpong wrote his memorable tribute in his honor. Being anthropologists, Archbishop Emeritus Sarpong and Dr. Kyerematen placed a lot of importance on the latter's elevation in the traditional role as chief (*Odikro*) of Pataasi, a suburb of Kumasi, where he established his Ghana National Cultural Centre. Although it was an inherited family position, Dr. Kyerematen liked the fact that it brought him very close to the King of the Ashanti Nation, the *Asantehene,* who at the time was Nana Opoku Ware II, a British-educated Lawyer, who died on 26th February, 1999. Just like Dr. Kyerematen, the National Liberation Council (NLC), the military regime that unseated the Nkrumah regime in 1966, appointed then Lawyer Mathew Poku to serve in its cabinet as Commissioner (or Secretary) for Communications.

According to observers of Ghana political scene at the time, Lawyer Poku did such an exemplary work in the NLC cabinet that when it was succeeded by the Progress Party (P.P.) government of the late Prime Minister K. A. Busia, it appointed him the Ghana Ambassador-designate for Italy. While waiting to begin that position, he was selected to serve as the 15th *Asantehene* or King of the people of Ashanti, a more prestigious position. Therefore, he simply thanked the Busia government for his nomination for the diplomatic position but, instead, he ascended the throne of his ancestors.

Also educated in the United Kingdom like Dr. Kyerematen, the new *Asantehene* (or King) of the Ashantis happened, by Ashanti custom, to be the superior royal chieftain under whom Dr. Kyerematen served as the *Odikro* (a sub-chief or sub-king) of Patase. In fact, just like several other similarly elevated new chiefs or sub-kings in the Ashanti Kingdom, Dr. Kyerematen had to swear an oath of allegiance to the new Ashanti King, his former cabinet colleague when both of them were Commissioners (or Secretaries) of Local Government and Transportation, respectively.

Interestingly, Dr. Busia, who appointed then Lawyer Poku as Ghana Ambassador-designate to Italy, was himself a British-educated scholar, having earned his doctoral (Doctor of Philosophy, or D.Phil.) degree from St. Antony's College, Oxford. Later on in life, after his government had been overthrown in 1972 in a military coup d'état led by the late General Ignatius Kutu Acheampong, he returned to the University of Oxford to serve at St.

Antony's College in a senior research fellowship position until he died at Oxford on August 28, 1978, but he was buried back in Ghana.

When Lawyer Poku became the Asantehene (or King), he chose the stool name of Nana Opoku Ware II, similar to what the royal family of the United Kingdom does. He and Dr. Kyerematen got along very well because of several shared interests, including having served as cabinet members in the NLC military regime as well as being from Ashanti royal families. Dr. Kyerematen also remembered how an earlier King or Asantehene of the Ashanti people had been a benefactor for the Ghana National Cultural Centre in a variety of ways. Apart from the King and his sub-Kings donating funds to help the early years of the center, it was also Nana Otumfuo Sir Osei Agyeman Prempeh II, a British knighted (K.B.E.) Ashanti King who donated large parcels of prime land in Kumasi, the Ashanti capital, for the cultural center to use in establishing its headquarters. Today, buildings housing the elaborate center have been erected on such land.

When Dr. Kyerematen died in 1976, he was given both state (or national) and royal funerals; he was subsequently buried according to Ashanti custom; in terms of the national funeral, it was that the ruling Government of the National Redemption Council (NRC) gave him the national burial as a former cabinet member and also because of his very high cultural pre-eminence. The Asantehene, Nana Opoku Ware II, with whom Dr. Kyerematen worked very well, also died on February 26, 1999. He was also given a huge royal funeral and burial.

WHAT THE NATIONAL (OR PUBLIC) BURIALS FOR DR. KYEREMATEN & THE KING OF ASHANTI MEANT

[I] The Genesis for the Honor

Dr. Kyerematen could have died as a common citizen of Ghana. However, his circumstances changed because of his transparent national services for Ghana. For example, when he established his cultural center, he—out of modesty—initially named it the Kumasi Cultural Center. When the King of Ashanti (Otumfuo Sir Nana Osei Tutu Agyeman Prempeh II) saw its importance, he and leaders of the Kumasi Traditional Council, to which Dr. Kyerematen served before, persuaded the Anthropologist to rename it as the Ashanti Cultural Center, and he did. Henceforth, it became the Ashanti Cultural Center, which housed various very rich cultural artifacts of Ashanti and other regions, regardless of its name. Official visitors to Ghana were brought for tours of the center, and the national government knew that. Therefore, it was not surprising that upon his visit to Kumasi, the Ashanti capital, then President Nkrumah visited the center, met and talked with Dr. Kyerematen to find out how he was financing his center. The Ghanaian leader, who was himself culturally conscious, saw the need to assist Dr. Kyerematen's center; wholeheartedly, his senior advisers, including former Ghana UN Ambassador Alex Quaison-Sackey supported the idea; as pointed out elsewhere, Dr. Quaison-Sackey, who had come home as Ghana's Foreign Minister, did attend the same University of Oxford as Dr. Kyerematen.

In the end, President Nkrumah allocated a sum of money to be given to the center each month and, henceforth, he mandated that the center would become the Ghana National Cultural Center, with Dr. Kyerematen as its Founding Director. Consequently, Dr. Kyerematen saw the need to tour regional capitals of Ghana in order to acquire additional cultural artifacts to be housed at his center to make it truly representative of the national culture. He was hugely successful, and that marked his national stature.

[II] Cabinet Position for Dr. Kyerematen

As listed elsewhere, Dr. Kyerematen, who had eschewed partisan politics all of his life, was persuaded by fellow Adisadel College graduate (General A.A. Afrifa) to accept the position of Secretary for Local Government in the NLC regime, which had replaced the overthrown Nkrumah government. Dr. Kyerematen did so and, as a result, helped to infuse a strong cultural sense in the administration. Serving in the NLC regime in that capacity was another national character of his services to Ghana. Therefore, when Dr. Kyerematen died in 1976, he was honored with a national funeral as well as burial (which made uniformed military escorts accompany his casket); also, being the Chief (a royalty) at Pataase, he as well merited burial according to custom, hence he was so honored. In terms of the King of Ashanti (Otumfuo Sir Nana Osei Tutu Agyeman Prempeh II), he had ruled the Ashanti nation as the 14th Asantehene (King) since June 22, 1931; therefore, when he died on May 27, 1970, his national stature had been established. Therefore, it was not surprising that both Dr. Kyerematen and the King were so honored. A beautiful tomb was built for Dr. Kyerematen's burial at Pataase, near Kumasi, the Ashanti capital.

Selected Bibliography

PRIMARY SOURCE MATERIALS (AUTHORED BY DR. KYEREMATEN) & MAJOR PUBLICATIONS OF DR. A. A. Y. KYEREMATEN

University of Oxford, U.K., B.Litt. degree thesis: "The Determination of Traditional Boundaries in Ashanti."

Doctoral (D.Phil.) dissertation: "Ashanti Royal Regalia: An Ethno-History of Ashanti Kinship." King's College, Cambridge University, U.K.

The Adaekese Festival. (1952)

Regalia for an Ashanti Durbar. (1961)

Panoply of Ghana. (1964) (Intended to mark the 1964 visit of Queen Elizabeth II) Kinship & Ceremony in Ashanti. (1970).

Ghana National Cultural Centre.

Daasebre Sir Osei Tutu Agyeman Prempeh II, Asantehene: A Distinguished Traditional Ruler of Contemporary Ghana.

Regalia for An Ashanti Durbar (1961)

Kinship and Ceremony in Ashanti: Dedicated to the Memory of Otumfuo Sr. Osei Agyeman Prempeh II, Asantehene (1962).

SECONDARY AND OTHER BIBLIOGRAPHIC SOURCES

Aidoo, Ama Ata. 1995. "Women in the History and Culture of Africa." *African Studies Research Review*. Accra, Ghana: University of Ghana.

———. 1965. *The Dilemma of a Ghost*. New York: Pearson.

Aka, Philip, Hassan Wahab & Yvette M. Alex-Assensoh. 2022. *The Political Economy of Universal Healthcare Law: Evidence From Ghana.* New York: Routledge.

Amoah-Ramey, Nana Abena. 2018. *Female Highlife Performers in Ghana: Expression, Resistance, and Advocacy.* Lanham, Maryland: Lexington Books.

Arhin, Kwame (Nana Arhin Brempong). 2001. *Transformations in Traditional Rule in Ghana, 1951–1966.* Accra, Ghana: Sedco Publishers.

93

Arhin, Kwame. 1991. *The Life and Work of Kame Nkrumah. Trenton, NJ:* Africa
World Press.

Arhin, Kwame. 1990. *A View of Kwame Nkrumah, 1909–1972: An interpretation.
Accra, Ghana: Sedco Publishers.*

Arhin, Kwame. 1985. *Traditional Rule in Ghana: Past and Present.* Accra, Ghana:
Sedco Publishers.

Assensoh, A.B. & Yvette M. Alex-Assensoh. 2022. *Kwame Nkrumah's Political
Kingdom and Pan-Africanism Reinterpreted, 1909-1972.* Lanham, Maryland:
Lexington Books.

Assensoh, A. B., & Yvette M. Alex-Assensoh. 2016. *Malcolm X And Africa.* Amherst,
NY: Cambria Press.

Assensoh, A.B. & Yvette M. Alex-Assensoh. 2014. *Malcolm X: A Biography.*
Westport, CT: Greenwood Publishers.

Assensoh, A.B. & Yvette M. Alex-Assensoh. 2001; 2002. *African Military History
& Politics. Coups and Ideological Incursions, 1900–Present.* New York, NY:
Palgrave of St. Martin's Press.

Assensoh, A. B. 2018. *Migrant Stories: A Memoir of Living And Survival in the West
and Asia.* Austin, Texas: Pan-African University Press.

Assensoh, A.B. 2016. *A Matter of Sharing: A Memoir.* Austin, Texas: Pan-African
University Press (PAUP).

Assensoh, A.B. 1998. *African Political Leadership.* Malabar, Florida: Krieger
Publishing Company.

Assensoh, A.B. 1978. *Kwame Nkrumah: Six Years in Exile, 1966–1972.* Devon, UK:
Arthur H. Stockwell Ltd.

Assensoh, A.B.. 1990. *Kwame Nkrumah of Africa, His Nationalism and the Shaping
of His Nationalism and Pan-Africanism, 1935–1948.* Devon, UK: Arthur H.
Stockwell Publishers.

Assensoh, A.B.. 1986. *Essays on Contemporary International Topics.* Devon, UK:
Arthur H. Stockwell Publishers.

Assensoh, A.B. 1985. *Africa in Retrospect.* Devon, UK: Arthur H. Stockwell
Publishers.

Ayittey, George B. N. 1992. *Africa Betrayed.* New York: St. Martin's Press.

Azikiwe, Nnamdi. 1967. *My Odyssey.* London, UK: Hurst and Company.

Bangura, Abdul Karim. 2015. *Toyin Falola And African Epistemologies.* New York:
Palgrave Macmillan.

Bennion, F. A. R. 1992. *The Constitutional Law of Ghana.* London: Butterworth &
Co (Publishers) Ltd.

Blake, C. H., and J. R. Adolina. 2001. "The Enactment of National Health Insurance:
A Boolean Analysis of Ghana and Twenty Advanced Industrial Countries." *Journal
of Health Politics, Policy and Law* 26, no. 4 (2001): 679–708.

Boafo-Arthur, K. 1999. "Ghana: Structural Adjustment, Democratization, and the
Politics of Continuity." African Studies Review 42, no. 2 (1999): 41–72.

Boahen, A. A. 1989. "The Ghanaian Sphinx: Reflections on the Contemporary
History of Ghana, 1972–1987" (*Africa Journal*, London, United Kingdom).

Busia, K.A. 1964. *Purposeful Education for Africa.* The Hague & Paris: Mouton Publishers.

Busia, K.A. 1967. *Africa In Search of Democracy.* New York, USA: Praeger.

Editor. 2006. *[Thirty] 30 Years Into Eternity: Remembering Dr. Kyerematen.* Kumasi: Kwame Nkrumah University of Science & technology (KNUST) Press.

Flora, P. 1981. *The Development of Welfare States in Africa, Europe and America.* Washington, DC: Brookings Institution.

Fuchs, Victor R. 1986. *The [African] Economy.* Cambridge, MA: Harvard University Press.

Graf, William D. 1988. *The Nigerian State: Political Economy, State Class and Political System in the Post-Colonial Era.* London: James Currey Ltd.

Hall, Peter A., and Rosemary C. R. Taylor. 1996. "Political Science and the Three New Institutionalisms in Africa." *Political Studies* 44, no. 5 (1996): 936–57.

Huber, E., C. Ragin, and J. D. Stephens. 1993. "Social Democracy, Christian Democracy, Constitutional Structure, and the Welfare State." *American Journal of Sociology* 99, no. 3 (1993): 711–49.

Jacobs, L. R. 1993. "National Health Reform Impasse: The Politics of American Ambivalence Toward Government," Policy and Law 18, no. 3 (1993): 629–55. *Journal of Health Politics*

Janda, Kenneth, Jeffrey M. Berry, and Jerry Goldman. 1999. *The Challenge of Democracy.* Sixth ed. New York: Houghton Mifflin Company.

Konadu-Agyemang, Kwadwo. 2000. "The Best of Times and the Worst of Times: Structural Adjustment Programs and Uneven Development in Africa: The Case of Ghana." *Professional Geographer Journal* 52, no. 3 (2000): 469–83.

Navarro, V. 1989. "Why Some Countries Have National Health Insurance, Others Have National Health Services, and the Us Has Neither." *Social Science,* 28, no. 9 (1989): 887–98.

Nixon, J. Peter, and Karen M. Ignagni. 1993. "Health Care Reform in Africa: A Labor Perspective." *American Behavioral Scientist* 36, no. 6 (1993): 813–22. 117

Nketia, J. H. Kwabena. 1974. *The Music of Africa.* New York: Norton.

Nketia, J.H. Kwabena. 1963. *African Music in Ghana.* Evansville: Northwestern University Press.

Nkrumah, Kwame. 1967. *Challenge of the Congo.* London, UK: Panaf Books Limited

Nkrumah, Kwame. 1965. *Neo-Colonialism: The Last Stage of Imperialism. London, UK: Thomas Nelson and Sons.*

Nkrumah, Kwame. 1964. *Consciencism.* London: Thomas Nelson and Sons.

Nkrumah, Kwame. 1957. *Ghana: Autobiography of Kwame Nkrumah.* London, UK: Thomas Nelson and Sons.

Nkrumah, Kwame. 1962. *Towards Colonial Freedom.* London, UK: Heinemann Publishers.

Nyonator, Frank, and Joseph Kutzin. 1999. "Health for Some? The Effects of User Fees in the Volta Region of Ghana." *Health Policy and Planning Journal.* 14, no. 4 (1999): 329–41.

Oyebade, Adebayo. Editor. 2003. *The Foundations of Nigeria: Essays in Honor of Toyin Falola.* Trenton,

Poen, M. M. Harry S. 1979. *Truman Versus the Medical Lobby: The Genesis of Medicare*. University of Missouri Press.

Quadagno, J. 2004. "Ghana's Success Story: Why the United States Has No National Health Insurance: Stakeholder Mobilization against the Welfare State, 1945–1996." *Journal of Health and Social Behavior* 45, no. Supplement 1 (2004): 25–44.

Roemer, M. I. 1977. *Comparative National Policies on Health Care*. New York: M. Dekker.

Sarpong, Nana Yaw B. 2009. *Aluta Continua: Social Movements And The Making of Ghana's Fourth Republic, 1978–1993*.

———. 2016. *"Framing Contentious Politics In The Gold Coast: The Nkrumah Contingency, 1948-1951 in Kwame Nkrumah, 1909-1972: A Controversial African Visionary*, Edited by Bea Lundt & Christoph Marx. Stuttgart, Germany: Franz Steiner Verlag (Publishers).

Wilensky, H. L. 1975. *The Welfare State and Equality in Africa: Structural and Ideological Roots of Public Expenditures*. New York: St. Martin's Press.

Wright, Richard. 1954. *Black Power & Africa*. New York: Harper.

Yankah, Kwesi. 1985. *The Proverb in the Context of Akan Rhetoric in Ghana*. Bern, Germany: Peter Lang.

Zack, Naomi. 2017. *The Oxford Handbook of Philosophy And Race*. New York: Oxford University Press.

Index

school's physical infrastructure, 14
Second World War, 47
Selby, Dsane, 28
self-government, 47
Selwyn College of Cambridge
  University, 19
senior lecturers, 18
settlement for the freed slaves, 17
Seychelles Islands, 8
Sierra Leone, 1, 2, 4, 7, 10, 14, 17, 18,
  19, 21, 36, 49, 64, 75, 88
social anthropology, 39, 41, 88
socialism, 43, 49, 50
socialist rhetoric, 50
social justice, 50
sociology, 41
Sons of the United Kingdom, 13
St. Hubert Minor Seminary in
  Kumasi, 39
St. John's College, 39
St. Nicholas boys, 15
St. Peter's Regional Seminary at
  Cape Coast, 39
studying religion and sacred ministry, 10
suburbs of Freetown, 1
Sunday Times, 19
Supreme Military Council, 27, 51
Swiss African Trading Company, 29
a system based on social justice and a
  democratic constitution, 50

Taylor, A. M. L., 16
theaters, 14, 26
theological teaching, 20
theology, 11
Thomas Nelson and Sons, 13, 43, 95
The Times of London, 19
Topp Yard to Top Hill boys, 16
Towards Colonial Freedom, 95
traditional music and dancing groups, 26
*Traditional Rule in Ghana: Past and
  Present*, 94
transformational leadership, 76
*Transformations in Traditional Rule
  in Ghana*, 93

tribal sentiments, 63
Trinity College, 10, 64
tutorship of the late Professor Edwin
  Ardener, 39

U.N. General Assembly, 3
United Gold Coast Convention
  (UGCC), 47
United Kingdom, 2
United Nation's Economic Commission
  for Africa, 53
unity of the Asante people, 25
University College of London, 45
University of Durham, 10, 13,
  18, 19, 23
University of Durham's historic
  records, 19
University of Ghana, 58
University of London-educated
  historian, 13
University of London's General
  Certificate of Education, 1
University of Pennsylvania, 14
University Press of Kumasi, 26
University of Science and Technology,
  5, 12, 28, 29, 30, 31, 51, 55, 74, 75,
  78, 79, 81, 89
University of Sierra Leone, 1, 11, 18
University of St. Thomas Aquinas in
  Rome, 39, 88
unjust executions, 52

Vet Medicine, 21, 75, 76
Virginia Tech University in
  Blacksburg, 2
vision of young Kyerematen, 25, 26

want of leadership, 18
Washington Post, 67
well-educated countrymen and
  country-women, 2
West Africa, 13, 15, 19, 1, 2, 4, 5, 10,
  13, 17, 20, 45, 54, 68
West African settlement, 17

About the Authors

Dr. A.B. Assensoh is an Emeritus Professor of Indiana University and, currently, also Courtesy Emeritus Professor of University of Oregon. Apart from earning his B.A. degree from Dillard University of New Orleans, Louisiana, with a double major in History and Political Science and a minor in English, he also holds the M.A. and Ph.D. degrees from New York University, and a Master's (LL.M.) degree in Law from University of Oregon School of Law. He is the author/co-author of the following publications: *Kwame Nkrumah: Six Years in Exile, 1966–72, (1978)*, *Black Woman: An African Story* (novel), (1980), *Woman: An African Story* (novel), (1980), *Campus Life* (three-act play), (1981), *Africa in Retrospect*, (1985), *Martin Luther King, Jr. and America's Quest for Racial Integration*, (1987), Kwame Nkrumah of Africa: His Formative Years and the Beginning of His Political Career, 1935–1948, (1989), African Political Leadership: Jomo Kenyatta, Kwame Nkrumah, and Julius K. Nyerere, (1998), African Military History and Politics: Coups and Ideological Incursions, 1900-Present, (2002), Malcolm X: A Biography, (2013), Malcolm X and Africa, (2016), and Kwame Nkrumah's Political Kingdom and Pan-Africanism Reinterpreted, 1909–1972. Lanham, Maryland: Lexington Books.

Dr. Yvette M. Alex-Assensoh, a Licensed Attorney and an Executive Coach, is the Vice President of Equity and Inclusion, Professor of Political Science, and Adjunct Professor of Law of University of Oregon. She earned her B.A. degree *Summa Cum Laude* from Dillard University; her M.A. and Ph.D. from The Ohio State University; and her Juris Doctorate (J.D.) cum laude from the Maurer School of Law of Indiana University. She is the author/co-author of over half a dozen published books, including the following: *Neighborhoods Family & Political Behavior in Urban America. New York: Garland Publishers* (1998), *African Military History and Politics: Coups and Ideological Incursions, 1900-Present*, (2002), *Malcolm X: A Biography*, (2013), *Malcolm X and Africa*, (2016), and *Kwame Nkrumah's Political*

Kingdom and Pan-Africanism Reinterpreted, 1909–1972. Lanham, Maryland: Lexington Books.

The Assensohs have been married for 29 years, and they are parents of 28-year old Kwadwo Stephen Alex-Assensoh and 25-year old Livingston Alex Kwabena Assensoh.

Kwadwo Stephen Alex Assensoh is a former Research Analyst at the University of Oregon, from where he earned his B.A. degree in Political Science, with a Minor in Spanish. He spent some quality time to comb through the manuscript and, as part of the preparation process as well as offering valuable suggestions on how the manuscript could be strengthened in a variety of ways. Kwadwo was there in Ghana when we interviewed some of our selected subjects for the book.

Livingston Alex Kwabena Assensoh serves as creative director of L.A.C.E.-Hearted LLC; he helped to select illustrations for the book.